WHAT SHE WANTS

DR. NEHA MEHTA

(PHD in Women Psychology)

Published By

Invincible Publication Pvt. Ltd.

Published by
Invincible Publication Pvt. Ltd.
201A, SAS Tower, Sector 38, Gurugram – 122003
Phone: +91-124-4034247, +91 9599066061
www.invinciblepublishers.com
Sales: Office No. 4760-61/23 Basement, Pratap Street,
Ansari Road, Daryaganj, Near ICICI Bank - 110002
Phone: +91-11-40198405
Email: invinciblepublishers@gmail.com

First edition – 2023

Book Name: What She Wants
ISBN: 978-93-58863-03-1

CONTENTS

PREFACE

In the nuanced tapestry of human relationships, the dynamics between men and women have often been likened to a complex puzzle, one that many claim is near-impossible to decipher. Yet, amid the seemingly enigmatic nature of women, I find solace in the notion that understanding isn't always the key; it's the appreciation, respect, and acknowledgment that truly matter. This is the cornerstone on which the narrative of this book rests.

It is a common refrain that comprehending a woman's mind is akin to unraveling an ancient scroll written in an unknown language. However, I posit a different perspective. Instead of attempting to unravel every nuance, let us embark on a journey to appreciate, celebrate, and nurture the essence of womanhood.

This book serves as a guide, not to unravel the intricacies of the female psyche, but to illuminate the path toward meaningful connection. It implores men not to focus on understanding, but rather on giving—give love, give respect, give a listening ear, and grant the space for her to exert the power of her essence. The simplicity of the game becomes apparent when we realize that the key lies not in deciphering a code but in embracing the basic tenets of love, respect, and reciprocity.

The lament often echoed by men, that women are elusive or demanding, stems from a perceived complexity that dissolves when approached with empathy. This book aims to bridge the gap by offering insights into what women truly desire. It dispels the notion that women are uninterested in nurturing relationships or families, showcasing the fallacy of stereotypes that often shroud the female experience.

From the personal to the professional, from birth to every subsequent step, this book meticulously explores the multifaceted dimensions of a woman's life. What brings her joy? What wounds her heart? What ignites her passion? These questions, and many more, find their answers within these pages.

It is crucial to recognize that women reciprocate what is bestowed upon them. Love begets love, respect begets respect. If one seeks only to extract power or intimacy without investing in the emotional bank account of love and respect, reciprocity becomes an arduous task for any individual, irrespective of gender.

Consider this preface not merely an introduction

but a handshake—a warm invitation to delve into the chapters that follow. A journey that spans from the rudiments to the profound, unveiling the myriad facets of a woman's mind, soul, and activities. A journey, I believe, that will leave you not only with newfound understanding but also with a profound appreciation for the intricacies that make each woman unique.

Should you wish to delve deeper or share your insights, I extend an open invitation to connect. This book is not just message to all people but a conversation starter, and I look forward to engaging with readers who, like me, seek to understand and appreciate the beauty of the feminine experience.

As you embark on this exploration, I encourage you to read the chapters sequentially, allowing the narrative to unfold organically, guiding you from 0 to 100 in the spectrum of understanding and appreciation.

In closing, if you find value in these pages, I eagerly anticipate your feedback. Let this be a communal journey, a dialogue that extends beyond these written words. Your thoughts, reflections, and shared experiences will enrich the tapestry we weave together.

With warm regards,

Dr. Neha Mehta

ACKNOWLEDGMENT

In the pursuit of strengthening the bonds that unite couples, “What She Wants” has emerged as a beacon guiding individuals toward deeper connections. This endeavor has been a collective effort, and I am profoundly grateful for the unwavering support and contributions that have paved the way for this book.

First and foremost, I express my deepest gratitude to God, my eternal source of strength and inspiration. I extend my heartfelt thanks to my parents on both sides, who have been pillars of love and encouragement throughout this journey.

To my husband, whose steadfast support has been a constant source of motivation, and my children, whose presence has been a source of joy and purpose, I offer my sincere appreciation. Your unwavering belief in my vision has made the path clearer and the destination more attainable.

I extend heartfelt gratitude to my dedicated team, whose commitment and hard work have been instrumental in bringing this vision to fruition. My mentors, who have played pivotal roles in my academic and professional endeavors, deserve special mention. Their guidance has been invaluable, shaping the trajectory of this project.

A profound acknowledgment is owed to Miss Sa Ian, a luminous presence throughout this journey. From editing to crafting, every word in this book bears the imprint of her dedication and expertise. Without her, this endeavor would not have been possible, and for that, I am truly grateful.

To the countless couples who have entrusted me with their stories, challenges, and aspirations over the past decade, your experiences have been the cornerstone of this work. The lessons learned and shared during counseling sessions have shaped the content of "What She Wants" into a reservoir of wisdom and practical insights.

This book stands as a culmination of the collective efforts of everyone involved—an amalgamation of experiences, knowledge, and heartfelt dedication. It is my sincere hope that the readers find resonance in these pages, as the essence of this book is a testament to the genuine collaboration and dedication of all those who contributed.

With deep gratitude,

Dr. Neha Mehta - PHD Women Psychology

Author - "What She Wants"

"UNLOCKING DESIRES: UNDERSTANDING WHAT WOMEN WANT"

INTRODUCTION

THE ENIGMA OF FEMALE DESIRES

Female desires are often viewed as a complex enigma, shaped by diverse influences. Their complexity is a result of a mix of biological, psychological, and societal factors. These desires can evolve over time, making them challenging to decipher. Societal norms and cultural expectations play a significant role in shaping women's desires. Historical roles and traditional gender expectations have contributed to the perplexity of female desires. Miscommunication and a lack of open dialogue further complicate the understanding of these desires.

Understanding the enigma of female desires is crucial for building healthier and more fulfilling relationships. It requires recognizing the multifaceted nature of these desires and fostering open communication. Empowering women to express their desires without fear of judgment is a vital step towards unraveling this enigma and creating more harmonious partnerships. In this quest to decode the enigma, it's essential to foster empathy, patience, and open-mindedness. Women's desires, like those of men, are unique to each individual. By embracing this diversity and seeking to understand, we can move beyond the enigma and build more meaningful connections.

The enigma of female desires is a topic that has confounded researchers, psychologists, and society for generations. Female desires are complex, multifaceted, and influenced by a myriad of factors, making them challenging to decipher. The enigma lies in the diverse and evolving nature of these desires, shaped by biological, psychological, and cultural influences. Societal norms and expectations, historical roles, and the often-fraught terrain of communication all contribute to the perceived complexity. Unlocking this enigma involves recognizing and celebrating the diversity of women's desires, fostering open communication, and empowering women to express their wants and needs without fear of judgment. In this exploration, we aim to shed light on the intricacies of female desires and promote a better understanding of this essential aspect of human nature.

Why Women's Desires Matter ?

Women's desires are of paramount importance, impacting their overall satisfaction and fulfillment. Understanding and addressing these desires can lead to increased happiness. They are a cornerstone of healthy relationships, fostering trust and communication between partners.

Acknowledging and fulfilling women's desires is not just vital on an individual level but also contributes to broader societal goals. It aligns with the principles of gender equality and female empowerment, breaking down traditional gender roles and expectations. Ignoring or suppressing women's desires can have adverse effects on their mental and emotional well-being. Recognizing and addressing these desires is fundamental for psychological health.

In a broader context, recognizing and addressing women's desires is a crucial step in achieving a more equitable and inclusive society. Women's desires matter not only on an individual level but also as a driving force for societal progress and harmony. As a society, we must value and respect these desires, acknowledging the integral role they play in shaping the world around us.

Women's desires matter profoundly, impacting individuals, relationships, and the broader societal landscape. Understanding and valuing these desires are essential steps toward building a more equitable and fulfilling world for all

Here is to Understand Why Women Desires Matter

- Women's desires matter for overall fulfillment and satisfaction.
- They are integral to the health and vitality of relationships.

- Acknowledging and fulfilling women's desires is fundamental to gender equality and female empowerment.
- Understanding and addressing these desires is crucial for psychological well-being.
- Women's desires play a key role in societal progress towards a more equitable and inclusive world.
- Pursuing one's desires fosters personal growth and development.
- Recognizing and supporting women's professional and economic aspirations contributes to career success and economic growth.

PART 1: UNDERSTANDING WOMEN'S DESIRES - WHAT A WOMAN IS?

I - Historical and Cultural Perspectives

In this chapter, we embark on a journey through time and across cultures to explore the intricate relationship between women's desires and the historical and cultural contexts that have shaped them. Understanding the roots of women's desires requires a deep appreciation of how societal expectations, roles, and norms have evolved over centuries and across different parts of the world.

To comprehend women's desires, we must first examine the historical landscape. Throughout history, women's roles and expectations have been subject to significant fluctuations. In ancient societies, women often played vital roles in their families, contributing to both economic and social well-being. As time progressed, particularly during the industrial revolution, women's roles evolved, largely moving from agrarian labor to the domestic sphere. The societal expectations placed on women have fluctuated as well.

In some cultures, women were celebrated as bearers of life, revered for their fertility and ability to nurture families. In contrast, others imposed rigid constraints on their behavior, restricting their desires and autonomy. The family unit, as the cornerstone of society, has been a focal point in shaping women's desires. Understanding how cultural norms surrounding marriage, motherhood, and familial roles have shifted is essential to appreciating the complexities of women's desires. The historical backdrop provides a lens through which we can better understand the desires of contemporary women, influenced by the collective history of their gender.

As we continue our exploration, we must recognize the critical role of cultural diversity in shaping women's desires. Different cultures around the world have distinct norms, values, and expectations, all of which have a profound impact on the desires of women within those societies.

The manner in which a culture perceives beauty, sexuality, and relationships can significantly influence women's desires. In some cultures, physical appearance and modesty may hold more significant sway, while in others, more liberated and diverse expressions of desires are embraced.

Additionally, traditions and customs play a pivotal role in guiding women's desires. Rituals, ceremonies, and familial expectations can mold the desires of women, sometimes steering them towards specific paths in life.

The modern world has seen a significant shift in the expectations placed upon women, with greater opportunities for education, careers, and self-determination.

Despite these changes, women's desires continue to be influenced by the legacies of their cultural and historical backgrounds. It's crucial to appreciate the interplay between the past and the present, as these influences shape the complexities of contemporary women's desires.

Ultimately, understanding the historical and cultural perspectives is essential in grasping the rich tapestry of women's desires. This knowledge provides a foundation for appreciating the diversity and individuality of these desires and lays the groundwork for the subsequent chapters that explore the intricacies of a woman's mind, body, emotions, and psychology in understanding what she truly desires in life.

Cultural Variations in Women's Desires to Understand

The impact of culture on women's desires extends to how these desires are expressed and understood. Different cultures may have diverse views on what is considered desirable, both in terms of physical attributes and behavioral expectations.

For instance, some cultures may place a high

value on modesty and discretion when it comes to discussing desires, while others may be more open and expressive. These variations affect not only how women communicate their desires but also how they perceive and understand them.

Moreover, cultural norms can shape ideals of beauty, body image, and fashion, which in turn influence women's self-esteem and desires. These cultural standards can have a significant impact on women's perceptions of themselves and what they find desirable in others.

Understanding these variations in cultural perspectives is vital in appreciating the complexity and diversity of women's desires around the world. It highlights the need for sensitivity and open-mindedness when engaging with women from different cultural backgrounds, as their desires may be deeply rooted in their unique cultural contexts.

II - The Mind and Female Desires

The Complex Landscape of Female Desires

In the intricate realm of female desires, the mind serves as a profound orchestrator. It is in the mind where passions are ignited, fantasies take shape, and the intricacies of attraction and intimacy are comprehended. To understand what a woman truly desires, it's essential to delve into the inner workings of her mind, which is a landscape rich with emotions, thoughts, and aspirations.

The mind plays a pivotal role in defining a woman's desires, influencing her choices, and molding her individuality. It's a dynamic force that interweaves with cultural, historical, and societal influences, creating a unique tapestry of what she seeks in life, relationships, and herself. This chapter embarks on a journey to explore the various facets of the female mind and its role in shaping desires.

The mind serves as the epicenter where the tapestry of a woman's desires is woven. It is not merely a passive observer but an active participant, influencing her choices, values, and preferences. This mental landscape is dynamic, continually evolving and responding to the myriad influences that shape a woman's life, including cultural, historical, and societal factors. In essence, a woman's desires are a reflection of her unique mental landscape, colored by her experiences, values, and emotions.

The Influence of Personal Experiences

A woman's experiences significantly mold her desires. Her journey through life, from childhood to adulthood, is marked by a series of experiences, both positive and challenging. These experiences contribute to the formation of her desires and can influence her preferences in profound ways.

Childhood experiences, family dynamics, friendships, and early romantic relationships all leave imprints on a woman's mind. These experiences often lay the foundation for her understanding of intimacy, love, and partnership. They can shape her expectations and desires in relationships, affecting her emotional connections and aspirations.

Moreover, positive experiences, such as supportive and nurturing relationships, can foster a sense of security and trust. Conversely, negative experiences, such as betrayals or heartbreak, can lead to emotional scars that influence her desires for intimacy, affection, and even the pursuit of self-fulfillment.

Societal and Cultural Influences

Societal and cultural influences are formidable forces that interact with a woman's mind, guiding her desires in a variety of ways. Cultural norms and societal expectations often shape the narratives surrounding what is considered desirable, affecting a woman's perception of herself, her body, and her role in relationships.

In some cultures, women may be encouraged to prioritize family and motherhood, which can deeply influence their desires for stability, emotional connection, and nurturing roles. In contrast, cultures that emphasize individualism and self-expression may lead women to seek desires related to personal growth, career achievements, or adventure.

Media and popular culture also play a substantial role in shaping women's desires. The portrayal of idealized beauty, romantic relationships, and success can affect how women perceive themselves and what they aspire to in their lives.

The Intricacies of Emotional Desires of Women

At the heart of a woman's desires lies a complex tapestry of emotions. Emotional desires encompass the yearnings for love, affection, emotional connection, and fulfillment. The mind, as the custodian of emotions, plays a central role in shaping these desires.

Women often seek emotional intimacy in their relationships, desiring open communication, trust, and a deep sense of connection with their partners. The mind, through its capacity for empathy and vulnerability, influences these desires, which are crucial for building and maintaining healthy relationships.

Moreover, the mind is where fantasies are born, fueling desires for romantic experiences, sexual exploration, and shared adventures. It's where dreams of passion, tenderness, and emotional fulfillment take shape, driving women to seek partners who can reciprocate and fulfill these desires.

In essence, "The Mind and Female Desires" explores the intricate interplay between a woman's experiences, societal influences, and the emotional landscape of her desires. It underscores the central role of the mind in shaping what a woman truly seeks in life and relationships, highlighting the need for empathy, communication, and self-awareness in understanding and fulfilling these desires.

III - The Body and Female Desires

Understanding the Physical Manifestation of Desires

The connection between a woman's body and her desires is intricate and deeply rooted in biology, psychology, and personal experiences. This chapter delves into the physical aspects of female desires, exploring the role of anatomy, hormones, and the physiological responses that influence what a woman craves in her relationships and intimate experiences.

A woman's body, with its complex network of nerves and hormones, plays a pivotal role in shaping her desires. Hormonal fluctuations, such as those occurring during the menstrual cycle, can influence her mood, arousal, and sexual preferences. Additionally, the physical experiences of pleasure, touch, and sensation contribute significantly to a woman's desires for intimacy and emotional connection.

Page 2:

The Influence of Body Image on Desires

The way a woman perceives her own body profoundly impacts her desires and self-confidence. Societal standards of beauty, often perpetuated by media and cultural influences, can create unrealistic expectations and lead to body dissatisfaction. Body positivity and self-acceptance are essential components in understanding female desires.

Negative body image can impact a woman's willingness to engage in intimate relationships, affecting her desire for emotional and physical connection. Addressing body image issues and promoting self-love are crucial steps in empowering women to embrace their desires and enjoy fulfilling relationships.

Page 3:

Sexual Health and Well-being

Sexual health is a fundamental aspect of a woman's overall well-being and desires. This section explores the importance of sexual education, awareness, and healthcare in nurturing a woman's desires. It covers topics such as reproductive health, contraception, and sexually transmitted infections, emphasizing the significance of informed choices and communication in intimate relationships.

A woman's sexual well-being is closely linked to her desires, encompassing both physical and emotional aspects. Addressing sexual health concerns, fostering open communication with healthcare providers, and understanding the various aspects of sexual well-being are vital for a woman to feel empowered in her desires and relationships.

Page 4:

Exploring Sensuality and Pleasure

The fourth page of this chapter delves into the exploration of sensuality and pleasure as integral components of female desires. Sensual experiences, including touch, taste, and scent, contribute to a woman's physical and emotional connection with her partner. Understanding her own body and discovering what brings her pleasure are key aspects of embracing her desires.

Exploration and communication within intimate relationships allow women to discover their preferences, boundaries, and fantasies. This openness and mutual respect create an environment where desires can be expressed, enhancing emotional intimacy and strengthening the bond between partners. This page emphasizes the importance of cultivating a positive and respectful approach to sensuality, pleasure, and the physical aspects of female desires.

Misconceptions about a woman people have

In a world shaped by evolving societal norms and expectations, women often find themselves battling against deeply ingrained misconceptions that cast shadows on their experiences and identities.

Stereotypes about women often limit their potential, perpetuating outdated expectations and reinforcing gender biases. By unraveling these myths, we embark on a mission to empower women to break free from the shackles of societal norms. The journey toward debunking these misconceptions is not only a testament to the resilience of women but also a call to challenge the status quo and pave the way for a more inclusive and equitable future.

As we delve into the multifaceted dimensions of women's lives, it becomes apparent that these misconceptions impact not only individual experiences but also societal perceptions at large. The narratives surrounding women's roles, abilities, and desires have far-reaching implications on how they navigate professional landscapes and intimate relationships. By critically examining and challenging these stereotypes, we endeavor to contribute to a transformative dialogue that recognizes the true depth and diversity of women's stories.

Beyond the confines of stereotypes, our exploration aims to spotlight the strength and agency inherent in women's experiences. By debunking misconceptions, we seek to amplify the voices of women who defy societal expectations, showcasing resilience, ambition, and the ability to forge authentic connections. In doing so, we aspire to foster a cultural shift that honors the unique contributions of women, dismantles preconceived notions, and ultimately cultivates an environment where individuals are free to embrace their true selves.

1: Emotional Misconceptions

1.1 Emotional Complexity:

In dissecting the prevailing misconception surrounding women's emotional complexity, it is imperative to delve into the intricacies of human emotion. Women, often unfairly labeled as overly emotional or irrational, grapple with a stereotype that portrays them as guided solely by sentiment. This oversimplification undermines the depth of women's emotional experiences, creating a disservice to their individuality. The reality is that women, like men, possess an intricate and diverse emotional spectrum that extends far beyond societal generalizations.

Women navigate emotions that encompass not only sensitivity but also resilience, strength, and nuanced understanding. This complexity allows them to respond to situations with a depth that defies stereotypes. Acknowledging the richness of women's emotional lives involves recognizing the multifaceted nature of their experiences. By debunking the myth of excessive emotionality, we open the door to a more nuanced understanding of women's responses, promoting empathy and dismantling harmful preconceptions that limit their emotional agency.

The path to debunking this myth lies in fostering a culture that encourages authentic emotional expression without judgment. By celebrating the diverse ways women experience and navigate emotions, we contribute to a more inclusive society that values individuality and recognizes the strength inherent in embracing the complexity of the human emotional experience.

1.2 Vulnerability and Strength:

Another pervasive misconception revolves

around the perceived vulnerability of women being equated with weakness. The stereotype that women are inherently fragile disregards the innate strength and resilience they demonstrate in the face of life's challenges. It is crucial to recognize that vulnerability is not a synonym for weakness; rather, it is a testament to one's courage in facing the complexities of life.

Debunking this myth involves challenging ingrained notions about the dichotomy between vulnerability and strength. Women's resilience, evident in various aspects of their lives, deserves acknowledgment and celebration. Their ability to navigate adversity, express vulnerability when needed, and emerge stronger is a testament to their inherent power.

Society, by debunking this myth, can foster a more compassionate understanding of women's emotional experiences. It requires dismantling stereotypes that undermine their strengths and perpetuate harmful biases. Embracing the complexity of women's emotional lives involves acknowledging both their vulnerabilities and strengths, creating a space for genuine understanding and appreciation of their multifaceted identities.

By challenging these misconceptions about women's emotional experiences, society can contribute to a more empathetic and supportive environment. Recognizing and celebrating the complexity, resilience, and strength inherent in women's emotions paves the way for a society that values authenticity and individuality, free from the constraints of limiting stereotypes.

Section 2: Mental Misconceptions

Intellectual Capacity:

A deeply ingrained and misleading stereotype contends that women possess an inherent intellectual inferiority compared to their male counterparts. This erroneous belief not only diminishes the countless achievements of women but also perpetuates biases that act as formidable barriers to their professional and personal growth. To dismantle this damaging misconception, a nuanced exploration into the diverse intellectual capacities of women is imperative. Challenging societal assumptions that underpin such harmful stereotypes is a crucial step in creating an inclusive space where the multifaceted talents of women are not only acknowledged but also celebrated.

Women, like men, contribute significantly to various intellectual fields, showcasing prowess and innovation across disciplines. From groundbreaking scientific discoveries to groundbreaking achievements in the arts, the rich intellectual tapestry of women defies the limitations imposed by stereotypes. By recognizing and celebrating the depth and diversity of women's intellectual contributions, society can recalibrate its perceptions, fostering an environment where women are not only seen as equals but are also encouraged to reach their full intellectual potential.

2. Mental Misconceptions

2.1 Intellectual Capacity:

A deeply ingrained and misleading stereotype contends that women possess an inherent intellectual inferiority compared to their male counterparts. This erroneous belief not only diminishes the countless achievements of women but also perpetuates biases that act as formidable barriers to their professional and personal growth. To dismantle this damaging misconception, a nuanced exploration into the diverse intellectual capacities of women is imperative. Challenging societal assumptions that underpin such harmful stereotypes is a crucial step in creating an inclusive space where the multifaceted talents of women are not only acknowledged but also celebrated.

Women, like men, contribute significantly to various intellectual fields, showcasing prowess and innovation across disciplines. From groundbreaking scientific discoveries to groundbreaking achievements in the arts, the rich intellectual tapestry of women defies the limitations imposed by stereotypes. By recognizing and celebrating the depth and diversity of women's intellectual contributions, society can recalibrate its perceptions, fostering an environment where women are not only seen as equals but are also encouraged to reach their full intellectual potential.

2.2 Decision-Making Abilities:

Linked closely to the misconceptions about intellectual capacity is the damaging belief that women are inherently indecisive or lack the ability to make sound judgments. In reality, women exhibit a broad spectrum of decision-making abilities, showcasing adaptability, critical thinking, and strategic acumen. Debunking this myth necessitates a deliberate effort to dismantle preconceived notions that unfairly hinder women from assuming leadership roles and making impactful choices.

Women's decision-making prowess is evident in various spheres of life, from boardrooms to households, where they demonstrate resilience and astuteness in navigating complex decisions. Challenging harmful biases that undermine women's decision-making abilities is not merely about rectifying an injustice; it is about unlocking the full potential of society by harnessing the diverse talents and perspectives that women bring to the table. By actively challenging these harmful biases, society can foster an environment where women are not only recognized for their decision-making capabilities but are also empowered to thrive in roles that demand strategic thinking and effective leadership.

Debunking mental misconceptions about women involves dismantling deeply ingrained stereotypes that limit their intellectual capacities and decision-making abilities. It requires a paradigm shift in societal attitudes, recognizing and celebrating the richness of women's contributions across various fields. By actively challenging these harmful biases, society can create an environment where women are not only seen as equals but are also encouraged to unleash their full potential, contributing to a more vibrant and inclusive intellectual landscape.

3: Intimate Misconceptions

3.1 Desire and Satisfaction:

In the intricate landscape of intimate relationships, persistent misconceptions cast a shadow over women's desires and satisfaction, depicting them as passive recipients rather than active participants.

Debunking this deeply ingrained myth necessitates a profound paradigm shift, one that acknowledges and affirms women's agency in expressing desires. It requires dispelling assumptions about their sexual preferences and fostering a culture of open communication to ensure mutual satisfaction.

Women, like their male counterparts, possess a rich and diverse array of desires that extend beyond societal stereotypes. Embracing this diversity involves recognizing that women actively contribute to the dynamics of intimate connections, expressing desires that are nuanced, complex, and uniquely their own. By dismantling the outdated notion of women as passive in intimate relationships, we pave the way for more fulfilling and equitable connections, where both partners actively participate in the co-creation of intimacy.

3.2 Orgasm Disparities:

Another prevalent misconception within the realm of intimacy revolves around the orgasm gap, perpetuating the erroneous belief that women inherently experience fewer orgasms than men. Addressing this complex issue demands a comprehensive approach. Dismantling societal taboos surrounding women's sexuality is a critical step, fostering an environment that promotes education about diverse sexual experiences. By creating spaces where women feel empowered to communicate their needs without judgment, we actively contribute to a more inclusive understanding of female sexuality.

Recognizing that factors such as communication, emotional connection, and self-discovery play pivotal roles in sexual satisfaction is crucial. By challenging these misconceptions, we dismantle harmful norms that contribute to the orgasm gap, fostering an environment where women can explore their desires freely and experience sexual pleasure without constraints.

3.3 Emotional Connection vs. Physical Desire:

A common dichotomy imposed on women suggests that they prioritize emotional connection over physical desire. This oversimplification neglects the intricate interplay between emotional and physical intimacy in women's lives. Debunking this myth requires acknowledging the fluidity of women's desires, understanding that emotional and physical connections are not mutually exclusive. By embracing the complexity of women's intimate desires, we move toward fostering relationships that honor both emotional and physical dimensions, free from restrictive stereotypes.

Women's desires are diverse and multifaceted, reflecting a spectrum that encompasses emotional and physical elements in varying degrees. Challenging the dichotomy imposed by societal norms allows for a more authentic exploration of intimacy, where women are free to express their desires without conforming to limiting expectations. By dismantling this myth, we contribute to the creation of relationships that celebrate the complexity of women's intimate lives, fostering an environment where individual desires are acknowledged, respected, and celebrated.

Debunking intimate misconceptions about women involves challenging deeply ingrained myths that impact their desires and satisfaction. It necessitates a cultural shift that acknowledges women as active participants in intimate relationships, fostering open communication and dispelling stereotypes. By embracing the complexity of women's intimate desires, we contribute to a more inclusive and fulfilling landscape where diverse expressions of intimacy are celebrated, and all individuals can experience satisfying and equitable connections.

4: The Impact of Media and Culture

4.1 Reinforcement of Stereotypes:

The pervasive influence of media and cultural narratives plays a significant role in perpetuating harmful misconceptions about women. From the romanticizing of unrealistic expectations to the reinforcement of traditional gender roles, these narratives contribute to a distorted understanding of women's roles in intimate relationships. Debunking these deeply ingrained myths necessitates a critical examination of media representations and a collective effort to reshape cultural narratives.

Media representations often depict women in stereotypical roles, portraying them as either damsels in distress or as passive recipients of romantic pursuits. Such depictions not only limit the understanding of the diverse experiences of women but also reinforce harmful gender norms. To challenge these prevailing misconceptions, there is a need for a broader spectrum of portrayals that reflect the complexity and agency of women in intimate relationships.

Advocating for more diverse and realistic portrayals of women in media becomes a crucial step in dismantling harmful stereotypes. This involves pushing for narratives that showcase women as active participants in their relationships, with desires, ambitions, and challenges that go beyond traditional tropes. By actively challenging these misconceptions, we contribute to a more accurate understanding of women's roles in intimate relationships, fostering a cultural environment that celebrates diversity and authenticity.

4.2 Empowering Narratives:

Counteracting detrimental stereotypes requires the active promotion of empowering narratives that authentically represent the diversity of women's experiences in intimate relationships. This involves highlighting stories that defy traditional norms and celebrate genuine expressions of desire, agency, and fulfillment. Empowering women to share their stories becomes a revolutionary act that challenges limiting misconceptions, fostering a cultural shift toward narratives that celebrate individuality and authenticity.

Media and cultural influences have the power to shape societal perceptions, and by actively promoting empowering narratives, we contribute to a more inclusive and nuanced understanding of women's roles in intimacy. Empowering narratives showcase women as dynamic individuals with a range of desires, challenges, and triumphs. These narratives not only provide more relatable and authentic representations but also empower women to embrace their unique identities within the context of intimate relationships.

Dismantling the impact of media and cultural narratives involves challenging deeply ingrained stereotypes about women's roles in intimate relationships. By critically examining and reshaping these representations, we pave the way for a more accurate and inclusive understanding. Advocating for diverse portrayals and empowering narratives becomes a collective effort to foster a cultural environment that celebrates the complexity and individuality of women in intimate relationships.

Strategies for Debunking Misconceptions

Education and Awareness:

Addressing pervasive misconceptions demands a concerted effort in education and awareness, with a particular focus on dismantling stereotypes related to women's lives. Implementing comprehensive sex education programs represents a cornerstone in this endeavor. These programs must go beyond the traditional narratives, encompassing a diverse range of experiences, desires, and relationships. By challenging ingrained beliefs through education, individuals can actively contribute to breaking down barriers and fostering a more inclusive environment.

Comprehensive sex education serves as a powerful tool in dismantling stereotypes by providing accurate information, fostering empathy, and encouraging critical thinking. It creates a foundation for a cultural shift, one that values the diversity of women's experiences. By equipping individuals with a nuanced understanding of sexuality, relationships, and gender dynamics, education becomes instrumental in challenging preconceived notions and contributing to a more informed and open-minded society.

Open Communication:

Creating a space for open communication is a pivotal strategy in debunking intimate misconceptions. Encouraging and normalizing dialogues about desires, boundaries, and expectations helps dismantle assumptions and fosters a deeper understanding between partners. Cultivating a culture of open communication within relationships and society at large is essential for dispelling myths and promoting healthy intimacy.

Open communication breaks down the barriers of silence and stigma that often shroud intimate topics. By fostering an environment where individuals feel comfortable expressing their desires, boundaries, and concerns, we contribute to breaking down misconceptions and creating more authentic connections. This involves not only acknowledging the importance of communication within individual relationships but also advocating for broader societal changes that destigmatize conversations around intimacy.

Representation Matters:

Representation plays a crucial role in reshaping societal perceptions and challenging ingrained stereotypes. Increasing the visibility of diverse women's experiences in media, literature, and popular culture is a potent strategy. By showcasing a broad spectrum of narratives, we can challenge stereotypes and foster a more accurate understanding of the complexities of women's lives.

Empowering women to share their stories becomes a transformative act that contributes to a collective narrative defying limiting misconceptions. Advocating for diverse and authentic representation involves pushing for changes in media and cultural norms. By actively participating in reshaping narratives, we contribute to a more inclusive society that celebrates the richness of women's experiences. This includes promoting narratives that showcase women as multifaceted individuals with diverse desires, aspirations, and challenges, thereby challenging limiting stereotypes and fostering a more inclusive cultural landscape.

These strategies collectively contribute to a comprehensive approach in debunking misconceptions about women. Through education, open communication, and a commitment to diverse and authentic representation, we can actively participate in reshaping societal attitudes and fostering a more inclusive and nuanced understanding of women's experiences.

IV - EMOTIONAL CONNECTION AND INTIMACY

Page 1

The Foundation of Emotional Intimacy

Emotional connection forms the cornerstone of meaningful and fulfilling relationships. This chapter explores the profound significance of emotional intimacy in the context of female desires. Emotional intimacy involves openness, vulnerability, trust, and mutual understanding, creating a safe space where desires can be expressed without fear of judgment or rejection.

At its core, emotional intimacy nurtures a sense of belonging and acceptance. When a woman feels emotionally connected to her partner, it enhances her feelings of security and allows her desires to flourish. This page emphasizes the importance of active listening, empathy, and shared experiences in building emotional intimacy, fostering an environment where desires can be acknowledged and celebrated.

Page 2:

Trust, Communication, and Vulnerability

Trust, communication, and vulnerability are essential components of emotional intimacy. Trust forms the foundation upon which emotional connection is built, enabling partners to share their desires openly. Effective communication ensures that desires are expressed clearly and understood, promoting understanding and empathy between partners. Vulnerability, while challenging, allows partners to connect on a deeper level, embracing each other's desires with acceptance and love.

This page explores the intricacies of building trust, improving communication skills, and embracing vulnerability within relationships. It highlights the role of active communication techniques, such as active listening and validation, in creating a supportive environment where desires can be openly discussed and respected.

Page 3:

Nurturing Emotional Intimacy in Relationships. How Important is that?

Emotional intimacy requires continuous nurturing and effort from both partners. This section discusses practical strategies for nurturing emotional connection and intimacy in relationships. It explores activities that promote bonding, such as shared hobbies, meaningful conversations, and acts of kindness. It also delves into the importance of mutual respect, appreciation, and validation in fostering a strong emotional connection.

Additionally, it emphasizes the significance of addressing conflicts and challenges in a healthy manner. Conflict resolution skills, empathy, and the ability to apologize and forgive are crucial elements in maintaining emotional intimacy. By addressing conflicts constructively, partners can strengthen their bond, allowing their desires to flourish in an environment of understanding and harmony.

This chapter explores the intersection of emotional intimacy and sexual desire. Emotional connection profoundly influences a woman's sexual desires and preferences. When a woman feels emotionally connected and secure in her relationship, it enhances her confidence, allowing her to express her desires more freely and explore her fantasies.

Emotional intimacy fosters a sense of safety and acceptance, enabling partners to communicate their sexual desires openly. Partners who are emotionally connected are more attuned to each other's needs and boundaries, enhancing the overall sexual experience. This page emphasizes the importance of creating a nurturing emotional environment where both partners can openly express their sexual desires, enhancing mutual satisfaction and strengthening their emotional bond.

V - PSYCHOLOGY OF FEMALE DESIRES

The journey through the psychology of female desires brings us to a fundamental realization — that a woman's sense of self-worth, influenced by societal expectations and her own self-perception, profoundly shapes what she desires in life and love. This connection between self-esteem and desires underscores the importance of fostering self-acceptance and self-love, as these serve as the bedrock upon which her authentic desires are built.

In the intricate tapestry of female desires, self-esteem acts as a guiding force. A woman's perception of her worthiness, both in her own eyes and within society, plays a pivotal role in the formation of her desires. This self-esteem is not solely confined to physical appearance; it extends to her self-concept, encompassing her talents, intelligence, and the value she places on her own happiness.

It's essential to recognize that societal norms and media influence the development of self-esteem in significant ways. Messages conveyed through advertisements, social media, and popular culture often perpetuate unrealistic beauty standards, which can lead women to question their own worthiness. These external influences can create an internal struggle where a woman feels pressured to conform to certain expectations rather than embracing her authentic self.

Body image, too, is a complex facet of the female psyche. A woman's body image is intrinsically linked to her self-esteem and, consequently, her desires. The perception of her physical self can either act as a catalyst or a hindrance to the fulfillment of her deepest desires.

The impact of a woman's body image on her desires extends to both intimate relationships and her broader life goals. When a woman feels confident in her own skin, she is more likely to express her desires openly, seek out experiences that bring her fulfillment, and embrace a sense of self-empowerment. Conversely, when body image is marred by insecurities, it can lead to self-doubt and reluctance in pursuing her desires, whether they are related to love, intimacy, or personal achievement.

The journey towards a woman's authentic desires involves addressing these self-esteem and body image issues with empathy and understanding. It necessitates acknowledging the profound impact of societal pressures on self-worth and self-acceptance. Encouraging women to celebrate their individuality, appreciating their unique qualities, and recognizing that their worth is not defined by external standards is a crucial step in the process of self-discovery and embracing desires.

Moreover, the realm of female desires is enriched by the presence of fantasies and imagination. These mental constructs, often deeply personal and emotionally charged, serve as gateways to what women truly crave in their lives. Fantasies may span a wide spectrum, from romantic daydreams to more adventurous or unconventional desires.

Understanding the role of fantasies in a woman's inner world is pivotal for nurturing healthy communication and exploration in relationships. It's essential to recognize that fantasies are not frivolous or shameful but are natural expressions of one's innermost desires. They offer a window into a woman's emotional landscape, reflecting her yearnings and longings. By embracing their fantasies and sharing them with their partners, women can create an open, supportive environment where desires can be expressed and explored without judgment or fear.

Fantasies also play a significant role in the realm of intimate desires. In romantic and sexual relationships, they serve as a source of inspiration and excitement, enriching the emotional and physical aspects of intimacy. Women who feel comfortable expressing their fantasies to their partners often find that their desires are not only acknowledged but celebrated. This mutual recognition fosters a deeper connection and intimacy, as partners explore and fulfill each other's desires in a spirit of shared adventure and exploration.

As we delve deeper into the psychology of female desires, it becomes evident that personal experiences and past traumas shape a woman's emotional landscape significantly. Both positive and challenging experiences leave indelible imprints on her psyche, influencing her desires in profound ways.

Positive experiences, such as nurturing and supportive relationships, lay the foundation for a woman's self-esteem and her desires for emotional and sexual connections. These experiences nurture a sense of self-worth and empowerment, enhancing her willingness to express her desires openly. Fulfilling achievements and moments of personal success further boost her self-esteem, reinforcing her belief in her capabilities and the worthiness of her desires.

On the other hand, traumatic experiences, such as past abuse or betrayals, can create emotional scars that linger and influence her desires. These experiences can lead to a hesitance in forming emotional connections and intimacy, as the fear of vulnerability and potential hurt looms large. Understanding the psychological impact of these experiences is essential in creating a supportive and empathetic environment within relationships.

Addressing these experiences with sensitivity and care can lead to healing and growth. Open communication, trust, and patience are vital in allowing women to confront their past traumas and embark on a journey towards fulfilling their desires. By creating safe spaces where women can share their experiences and their emotional journey, partners can play a crucial role in helping each other heal and move forward with strength and resilience.

Societal and cultural influences wield substantial power in shaping the psychology of female desires. Media, advertising, and societal narratives play pivotal roles in constructing a woman's perception of beauty, relationships, and success. These external influences often perpetuate unrealistic standards and ideals that can create feelings of inadequacy and pressures to conform.

Understanding the role of these influences and their impact on a woman's psychology is pivotal in comprehending the complexities of female desires. Women find themselves navigating through a landscape of societal expectations, where conformity to certain norms can overshadow the pursuit of their own authentic desires.

It's important to recognize that societal and cultural influences are not inherently negative, but they can become problematic when they lead to unrealistic expectations and hinder self-acceptance. Empowering women to resist the pressures of conformity and discover their authentic desires is an essential step in their journey of self-discovery. It calls for encouraging women to question and challenge societal norms, embrace their individuality, and forge their own paths to fulfillment.

The intersection of desire and identity is where a woman's psychological landscape converges with her self-identity, values, and personal goals. A woman's desires are closely intertwined with her sense of self, representing her most genuine wants and needs. Navigating this intersection involves understanding how a woman's desires align with her identity and how they contribute to her sense of self-fulfillment.

In this journey, it's vital to emphasize the importance of embracing desires that align with a woman's true self and values. Authenticity becomes the guiding star, and women are encouraged to express their desires without fear of judgment or condemnation. Open and empathetic communication in relationships is key, creating a space where desires can be openly discussed, explored, and fulfilled while maintaining authenticity and respect for one's identity.

The intersection of desire and identity represents a deeply personal journey for each woman. It is where they reconcile their desires with their sense of self, finding the balance between what they yearn for and who they genuinely are. This process is often ongoing and evolving, as women grow and change, and their desires adapt to new experiences and understandings.

Understanding the intricate psychology of female desires is fundamental to appreciating the depth and diversity of women's aspirations. It underscores the need for self-acceptance, open communication, and a supportive environment in personal and intimate relationships. **Women's desires are not static; they evolve, adapt, and grow as they continue their journey of self-discovery.** This chapter emphasizes that a woman's psychology is the foundation upon which her desires are built, urging her to explore and embrace her authentic desires with confidence and self-assuredness.

In the quest to fathom the psychology of female desires, it becomes evident that a woman's emotional world is a dynamic tapestry of intricacies and subtleties. It's a terrain where emotions, thoughts, and experiences converge to create a unique psychological landscape that influences her deepest yearnings.

The journey through the psychology of female desires brings us to a fundamental realization — that a woman's sense of self-worth, influenced by societal expectations and her own self-perception, profoundly shapes what she desires in life and love. This connection between self-esteem and desires underscores the importance of fostering self-acceptance and self-love, as these serve as the bedrock upon which her authentic desires are built.

Fantasy and imagination are essential companions on this journey, igniting the flames of desire. Whether romantic, sensual, or adventurous, fantasies offer a glimpse into a woman's innermost desires. Understanding the role of fantasies in her emotional world is crucial for fostering open and honest communication in her relationships. When a woman feels safe sharing her fantasies with a partner, it creates a space where desires can be explored without judgment or fear.

The complex landscape of female desires

is also shaped by personal experiences and past traumas. Positive experiences, such as nurturing relationships or personal achievements, can bolster a woman's self-esteem and her desires for emotional and sexual connections. Understanding how these experiences contribute to her desires is essential for creating supportive and empathetic relationships. Traumatic experiences, on the other hand, can create emotional scars that influence her ability to express and explore her desires. Addressing these experiences with empathy, open communication, and patience is crucial in fostering a supportive environment in relationships.

Societal and cultural influences play a significant role in shaping the psychology of female desires. Media, advertising, and societal narratives impact a woman's perception of beauty, relationships, and success. Cultural norms and expectations contribute to a woman's understanding of her role in her community and relationships. Navigating these influences and their impact on a woman's psychology is crucial in understanding the complexities of female desires. Empowering women to resist the pressures of conformity and discover their authentic desires is essential in their journey of self-discovery.

The intersection of desire and identity is where a woman's desires align with her self-identity, values, and personal goals. Embracing desires that align with a woman's true self and values is essential. Open and empathetic communication in relationships creates a space where desires can be expressed, explored, and fulfilled while maintaining authenticity and respect for one's identity. Understanding the intricate psychology of female desires is fundamental to appreciating the depth and diversity of women's aspirations. It underscores the need for self-acceptance, open communication, and a supportive environment in personal and intimate relationships. Women's desires are not static; they evolve, adapt, and grow as they continue their journey of self-discovery.

This comprehensive exploration of the psychology of female desires underscores that the mind and emotions are central to understanding the depths of what a woman truly craves. It's a journey that delves into the rich tapestry of a woman's psyche, where emotions, thoughts, and experiences coalesce to form the foundation of her desires. As women continue their odyssey of self-discovery, they unravel the intricate connections between self-esteem, body image, fantasies, experiences, societal influences, and the alignment of desires with their true identity. This journey is one of empowerment, embracing authenticity, and nurturing relationships that encourage women to express and fulfill their desires with confidence and self-assuredness.

PART 2: WHAT WOMEN WANT IN RELATIONSHIPS ?

I - Communication and Trust

In the world of relationships, women desire some fundamental elements that resonate deeply with their wants and needs. At the core of these desires lies the foundation of every successful and thriving relationship: communication and trust. This chapter delves into what women genuinely want in a relationship and why communication and trust are the cornerstones of their hopes and expectations.

Human beings, regardless of gender, have a universal need for connection and companionship. Women are no exception. What women want in a relationship is a longing for a real connection, a bond that goes beyond the surface and delves into understanding each other emotionally. They wish for partners who actively listen, who value meaningful conversations, and who make them feel important in the relationship. Open and honest communication is the first step in creating an environment where women feel loved and understood.

Effective communication acts as a bridge that connects two individuals, helping them navigate the challenges that often arise in relationships. Women desire partners who can communicate clearly, with empathy, and active engagement. They appreciate when their partners express themselves and actively seek to understand their thoughts and emotions. Communication isn't just about words; it also includes non-verbal cues and gestures that show love, care, and support, such as a reassuring touch or a loving smile.

Open and honest communication is closely linked to creating a safe space within a relationship. Women want an environment where they can express their thoughts and emotions freely, without the fear of judgment or rejection. This safe space allows them to share their desires, dreams, and vulnerabilities without holding back. Partners who create these safe spaces allow women to be their true selves, understanding that being open and vulnerable is not a sign of weakness but an expression of trust and intimacy. The ability to share fears, insecurities, and dreams is a hallmark of a relationship where communication flows freely.

Empathy is crucial to understanding, and women desire partners who can empathize with their thoughts and emotions. Partners who understand the importance of validating a woman's emotions and experiences create a sense of trust and emotional closeness. This validation involves recognizing that her feelings are real and significant, even if they differ from one's own.

Trust is the solid foundation of any successful relationship. Women crave deep and unwavering trust, which covers all aspects of their partnership, from emotional security to fidelity. Trust is nurtured through honesty, integrity, and reliability. Women appreciate partners who keep their promises, are transparent about their feelings and actions, and remain loyal in their commitment to the relationship.

Past experiences, including betrayals or broken trust, can have a significant impact on a woman's need for emotional safety. Partners who understand these past experiences and provide the support and patience required for healing demonstrate their trustworthiness and commitment to a relationship where trust is rebuilt and protected. Transparency and honesty are essential in creating an environment where there are no hidden agendas or concealed truths.

Reliability and consistency are also important aspects of trust. Women seek partners who are dependable and can be counted on in both good times and bad. This reliability extends to promises, commitments, and being there in times of need. Consistency in behavior, attitude, and emotional support fosters a sense of emotional security.

Trust significantly influences a woman's emotional well-being in a relationship. A relationship built on trust provides emotional safety, allowing women to express their thoughts, desires, and vulnerabilities without hesitation. In an environment of trust, women are more likely to share their deepest desires and explore their fantasies, knowing that they will not be judged or rejected. This trust creates a space for the free expression and fulfillment of desires, enhancing intimacy and connection within the relationship.

Establishing and respecting boundaries is an integral part of trust. Boundaries serve as the framework that defines the limits and expectations within a relationship. Women want partners who respect their boundaries and also communicate their own. Respecting boundaries is a manifestation of trust and respect for each other's autonomy and individuality, allowing women to flourish within the relationship.

Challenges and conflicts are inherent in any relationship. Women value partners who engage in open and constructive communication when conflicts arise. When partners approach challenges collaboratively and constructively, it fosters a deeper sense of trust and emotional closeness within the relationship.

The Healing Power of Trust

Trust not only serves as a foundation for a healthy

relationship but also as a catalyst for healing and growth. It provides a safe space where women can overcome past wounds and traumas, knowing that their partner stands firmly by their side. This healing power of trust allows women to shed their emotional burdens, fostering a deeper connection and a newfound sense of wholeness within the relationship.

The Dance of Vulnerability

Vulnerability is a courageous act of trust. When women feel safe within a relationship, they are more willing to open up and reveal their true selves. This vulnerability deepens the emotional connection, allowing partners to explore desires, fantasies, and emotions that were once kept hidden. It's within this dance of vulnerability that the most profound aspects of a woman's desires are uncovered and celebrated.

A World of Shared Dreams

In a relationship rooted in trust, women find a partner with whom they can build a world of shared dreams. These dreams encompass not only their personal aspirations but also the desires they hold for the relationship itself. Women want to co-create a future where their desires are not only acknowledged but actively pursued, ensuring that both partners thrive in a relationship that celebrates their individuality.

Fulfilling Desires, Nurturing Love

Ultimately, what women want in a relationship is the ability to fulfill their desires while nurturing a deep and lasting love. It's a dynamic interplay of trust and communication that allows them to explore their innermost desires without fear, knowing that their partner will stand beside them every step of the way. This fulfillment extends beyond the physical realm, touching the emotional and psychological aspects of their desires, ultimately leading to a love that grows stronger with each passing day.

The essence of what women want in a relationship goes beyond mere words; it's a profound connection and an unshakable trust that create an environment where desires are not only acknowledged but embraced. This deep understanding and unwavering support allow women to explore the multifaceted landscape of their desires, unveiling a world of possibilitics where their aspirations are not only met but celebrated.

This celebration of desires is a testament to the strength and resilience of a relationship built on trust and open communication. It's a journey where emotional bonds deepen, trust strengthens, and love flourishes, leading to a profound sense of fulfillment and happiness that knows no bounds.

In summary, a relationship that fulfills a woman's desires is a space of trust and open communication where she can explore her innermost aspirations and vulnerabilities without fear. It's a journey of shared dreams, healing, and the celebration of desires, ultimately leading to a love that stands the test of time and grows stronger with each passing day.

II - Love, Affection, and Emotional Fulfillment

Love takes on a multitude of forms in a woman's life. It begins with self-love, the foundation upon which all other forms of love are built. Self-love is the essential cornerstone of emotional fulfillment, allowing a woman to embrace her worth and value.

The love shared with a partner is a unique and profound experience. It's the romantic love that ignites passions, fosters intimacy, and creates a deep emotional bond. A loving partnership is a haven where a woman can fully express herself, knowing that she is cherished and valued.

Beyond romantic love, there's the unconditional love for family. The bonds of mother, daughter, sister, and friend provide emotional support and a sense of belonging. These relationships are sources of love, comfort, and strength, enriching a woman's life.

Affection is love's gentle expression in everyday life. It's the warmth of a hug, the softness of a kiss, and the reassurance of a touch. Affection is conveyed through the smallest gestures, yet it carries immense significance in a woman's emotional landscape.

The goodnight kisses, the surprise "I love you" messages, and the comforting presence of a partner during difficult times are all manifestations of affection. These acts of tenderness create an environment of emotional security, reminding a woman that she is cherished.

Emotional fulfillment is the realization of being emotionally whole within a relationship. It's the profound sense that one's emotional needs are not just met but exceeded. Emotional fulfillment is a testament to the depth of understanding and emotional connection shared with a partner.

Partners who actively engage in conversations that go beyond the surface create emotional intimacy. They listen without judgment, offer unwavering support during times of vulnerability, and share in both the joys and challenges of life. This emotional connection is the cornerstone of fulfillment.

The interplay of love, affection, and emotional fulfillment creates a powerful connection between partners. It's a bridge that allows a woman to share her deepest desires, fears, and aspirations. Partners who nurture this connection build a strong emotional foundation, capable of withstanding the tests of time.

Within this connection, love is expressed not only through words but also through actions. It's the partner who remembers her favorite song, the surprise date nights, and the handwritten love notes left in unexpected places. These expressions of love enhance the emotional bond between partners.

Nurturing emotional well-being is a shared responsibility within a relationship. It involves self-care and mutual support during challenging times. Partners who prioritize emotional well-being provide the foundation for a woman to flourish, both as an individual and within the relationship.

Self-care includes acknowledging one's own emotional needs and communicating them to a partner. It's a dialogue that ensures both partners actively engage in supporting each other's emotional well-being. It's the mutual understanding that emotions are complex and ever-evolving, and being there to navigate them together.

Love, affection, and emotional fulfillment are closely intertwined with trust and emotional security. When a woman feels loved and cherished, trust deepens, providing emotional security. This security creates an environment where she can openly express her desires and vulnerabilities, fostering emotional fulfillment.

In a relationship built on trust, partners share their innermost thoughts and desires. They create a space where fears and insecurities can be unveiled without judgment. The trust built through open communication and unwavering support is the foundation of emotional security.

Love Language is all you need to understand!!

Understanding a **woman's love language** is vital for nurturing love, affection, and emotional fulfillment. Everyone has their unique way of feeling loved and expressing love. Partners who grasp each other's love languages can customize their gestures and actions to create an environment of emotional fulfillment.

In this mutual understanding, love becomes a shared language. Partners become attuned to each other's needs, expressing love in ways that resonate deeply. It's a dance of reciprocity, where both partners actively contribute to sustaining love, affection, and emotional fulfillment.

The impact of love, affection, and emotional fulfillment extends beyond the boundaries of the relationship. These elements influence a woman's overall well-being, including her mental and physical health. Partners who actively contribute to these aspects not only fulfill her desires but also create a life filled with love, happiness, and fulfillment.

In essence, love, affection, and emotional fulfillment are at the core of a woman's desires within a relationship. They create a profound emotional landscape where she can thrive, express her desires, and build a lasting bond with her partner. Love, in all its forms, nourishes the soul and becomes the foundation upon which an enduring relationship is built.

Within a loving relationship, physical affection plays a significant role in nurturing the emotional bond between partners. Physical affection goes beyond the act of sex; it encompasses the power of touch, cuddling, and physical closeness. These gestures of physical love create a sense of emotional connection and intimacy.

The touch of a hand, the embrace of a hug, and the tenderness of a kiss are all expressions of physical affection. They convey a depth of emotion that words often cannot. Physical affection is the unspoken language of love, a testament to the intimate connection shared by partners.

Is Sexual Intimacy Important in a Woman's Life?

Sexual intimacy is a vital component of love and affection in a romantic relationship. It's the physical expression of desire and a unique form of bonding between partners. A healthy sexual relationship enhances emotional fulfillment, deepening the connection between a woman and her partner.

Partners who prioritize sexual intimacy understand that it's not just a physical act but a profound emotional experience. It's the understanding that intimacy extends beyond the bedroom, creating a closeness that goes beyond words. In a fulfilling sexual relationship, partners explore each other's desires, fantasies, and needs, creating a sense of fulfillment.

The intertwining of love, affection, and sexual intimacy creates a harmonious balance that satisfies a woman's emotional desires. It's the recognition that love is not just an abstract concept but a tangible force that fills the heart. Affection becomes a daily reminder of love's presence, and sexual intimacy solidifies the emotional connection.

The emotional connection within a relationship extends to shared dreams and aspirations. A woman's desires often encompass more than just emotional and physical aspects; they include a vision for the future. Partners who actively engage in building a shared vision create a deep sense of fulfillment.

Shared dreams involve not only personal goals but also collective aspirations as a couple. It's the journey of co-creating a life together, one filled with adventures, challenges, and accomplishments. Partners who work together to fulfill these dreams contribute to a woman's emotional well-being.

A relationship's ability to adapt and grow in the face of challenges is a testament to its strength. Life presents obstacles and difficulties, and partners who navigate these challenges together create a bond that deepens love and emotional fulfillment. Resilience in the face of adversity strengthens the emotional connection between partners.

Nurturing Relationships - How important is that?

In a nurturing relationship, emotional fulfillment is not stagnant; it evolves and grows over time. It's the understanding that love, affection, and shared dreams are not static but ever-changing. A woman's desires adapt as she experiences different phases of life, and partners who continue to support her emotional well-being create lasting emotional fulfillment.

The understanding of emotional well-being extends to self-love. A woman's ability to love and cherish herself is the foundation upon which all other forms of love are built. Partners who encourage self-love and self-care enhance a woman's emotional fulfillment.

Self-love includes practices that prioritize personal well-being, both physically and mentally. It's acknowledging one's worth and treating oneself with kindness and respect. Partners who support self-love understand that a woman's emotional fulfillment begins with a strong sense of self-worth.

Love is not limited to words indeed!!

Love in a relationship is not limited to words; it's also expressed through actions. Small gestures of love, like preparing a favorite meal, leaving surprise notes, or simply spending quality time together, play a vital role in fulfilling a woman's emotional desires. These actions reinforce the love and affection partners share.

A deep emotional connection is further strengthened through the process of active listening. Partners who truly listen and understand each other create an environment where emotional fulfillment thrives. It's the ability to communicate without judgment, to validate feelings, and to provide emotional support. This empathetic connection fosters emotional intimacy, allowing a woman to express herself without reservation.

Partners who actively engage in building emotional intimacy understand that it's a continuous journey. It involves learning about each other's likes, dislikes, fears, and aspirations. As partners explore these facets of each other, they create a deeper bond that contributes to emotional fulfillment.

Empathy and emotional connection also extend to shared experiences. Engaging in activities together, whether it's traveling, pursuing hobbies, or simply enjoying a movie night, deepens the emotional connection between partners. These shared experiences create lasting memories and a sense of togetherness, fulfilling a woman's emotional desires.

Partners who actively acknowledge and celebrate each other's achievements and milestones contribute to emotional fulfillment. Recognizing and applauding each other's successes, no matter how small, nurtures a sense of validation and emotional connection. It's the understanding that partners are each other's biggest cheerleaders.

Emotional fulfillment also involves respecting each other's autonomy and individuality. Partners who allow space for personal growth and self-expression contribute to a woman's sense of self-worth. It's the knowledge that she is loved and cherished for who she is as an individual, fostering emotional well-being.

Emotional safety within a relationship is paramount. Women desire partners who provide a secure emotional environment where they can express their fears, insecurities, and vulnerabilities without fear of judgment. Partners who offer this safety demonstrate their commitment to nurturing emotional fulfillment.

Understanding a woman's emotional desires involves recognizing the importance of validation. Partners who acknowledge and validate a woman's emotions, even when they differ from their own, create a sense of trust and emotional closeness. This validation involves understanding that her feelings are real and significant.

Communication in a fulfilling relationship goes beyond everyday conversations. Partners who engage in deep, meaningful dialogues about life, love, dreams, and desires build emotional intimacy. These conversations contribute to a woman's emotional fulfillment, as they foster understanding and connection.

The expression of love is not limited to grand, elaborate gestures. Small, everyday acts of kindness and love, like making a cup of tea, offering a comforting hug, or simply being there during challenging times, are significant. Partners who consistently engage in these acts create a loving and emotionally fulfilling environment.

In a relationship filled with love, affection, and emotional fulfillment, there is room for growth and evolution. As time passes, partners continue to adapt to each other's changing desires and needs. The ability to embrace change and grow together leads to an enduring emotional connection that stands the test of time.

III - Commitment and Long-Term Partnerships

The Essence of Commitment to Explore

Commitment is the bedrock upon which lasting love is built. For women, it signifies the unwavering dedication to nurturing and safeguarding the relationship. This chapter will begin by dissecting the essence of commitment, exploring what it truly means and why it is the fundamental building block of a strong and enduring partnership.

Commitment in a relationship goes beyond simply being together. It represents the promise to invest time, effort, and emotions in building a shared future. It's the willingness to stand by each other's side through the highs and lows, and it's the foundation on which trust, love, and intimacy thrive. Commitment is the assurance that both partners are working toward a common goal, which is to nurture a loving, lasting connection.

To understand the role of commitment in long-term partnerships, it's essential to recognize its evolution. Commitment doesn't remain stagnant but deepens as the relationship progresses.

At the start of a relationship, commitment is often about the decision to be together. It's a promise to be exclusive and devoted to each other. However, as the relationship matures, commitment extends to encompass the practical aspects of life, such as sharing finances, building a home together, or raising a family. It transforms into a mutual understanding that both individuals are in it for the long haul, through thick and thin.

A shared vision is like a roadmap for the relationship, guiding both partners toward a future they both desire. When a couple shares common goals and dreams, it creates a strong sense of togetherness. It's not just about discussing individual aspirations but about finding a way to merge those aspirations into a vision that benefits both partners. This shared vision becomes a source of motivation, encouraging them to stay committed to each other and the future they're building.

For example, consider a couple, Sarah and John. When they first met, they were both ambitious professionals with dreams of success in their respective careers. They decided to merge their dreams into a shared vision by supporting each other's career goals and discussing how they could balance their personal aspirations with their life together. This shared vision became their driving force, a commitment to helping each other succeed.

Is Emotional Security an Important Factor?

Emotional security is like a warm, comforting embrace that envelops the relationship. It's the feeling of being truly seen, heard, and understood. In a committed partnership, emotional security is the invisible safety net that allows women to express their desires, thoughts, and feelings without fear of judgment.

Consider the case of Emily and Daniel, a couple that faced a challenging situation. Emily lost her job, and they had to rely on Daniel's income for a while. In this difficult period, Daniel assured Emily that they were in this together and that her worth wasn't tied to her job. He provided the emotional security she needed during a vulnerable time, reinforcing their commitment.

Trust and commitment are closely intertwined. A commitment to maintaining trust within the relationship ensures that women can confide their desires and vulnerabilities without fear.

For instance, imagine Lisa and Mark, a couple that went through a period of long-distance due to work commitments. Trust was vital in maintaining their commitment. Mark consistently communicated with Lisa, reassuring her of his dedication despite the physical distance. His trustworthiness was a testament to his commitment, and it allowed Lisa to share her feelings, desires, and insecurities openly.

Life isn't a smooth sailing journey, and women understand this. What they seek in a committed partnership is a companion who will weather the storms with them.

Lets Consider another example of Alex and Maria. They faced a significant challenge when Maria's mother fell seriously ill. Alex didn't shy away from the situation but took on caregiving responsibilities alongside Maria. Their commitment to each other and their shared resilience allowed them to navigate this difficult period, ultimately strengthening their bond.

Resilience is the relationship's ability to adapt and bounce back from difficulties. In a committed partnership, resilience is nurtured through open communication, trust, and a shared commitment to surmounting obstacles together. Resilience means that no matter what life throws your way, you emerge from the experience stronger and even more committed to each other.

The Role of Communication in Understanding Women

Effective communication is vital in a committed partnership. Women want partners who are open to discussing the intricacies of the relationship, addressing concerns, and being receptive to each other's needs and desires.

Consider the story of Sarah and Michael. They maintained open communication channels by having regular relationship check-ins. They would sit down to discuss their feelings, concerns, and desires, which allowed them to address issues as they arose. Effective communication was the tool that helped them navigate the complexities of their long-term partnership and keep their connection strong.

Celebrating Milestones with your Partner!

Milestones, whether big or small, play a significant role in reinforcing commitment. Partners who commemorate anniversaries, achievements, and shared moments create a sense of appreciation and commitment.

For instance, David and Jessica celebrated their anniversary by revisiting the place where they had their first date. They also celebrated personal achievements, like Jessica finishing her degree and David receiving a promotion at work. These celebrations were not only a testament to their commitment but also a way to create lasting memories and reinforce their bond.In a committed partnership, personal growth is encouraged and celebrated. It's about supporting each other's individual dreams and aspirations. Commitment doesn't mean losing one's identity within the relationship; it means growing both as a couple and as individuals.

Commitment and long-term partnerships are the crucible in which lasting love is nurtured. Women desire the security, emotional fulfillment, and the unwavering support that committed relationships provide. They seek partners who are dedicated to building a shared vision, who offer emotional security, and who are willing to weather life's storms together. In the end, commitment fosters resilience, open communication, and the celebration of milestones, all while allowing room for personal growth. It's a journey that, when navigated hand in hand, leads to a love that deepens and thrives over time.

Commitment and long-term partnerships are central to what women want in relationships. A strong, committed relationship offers a sense of security, trust, and emotional fulfillment. It's about creating a shared vision for the future, nurturing a love that grows with time, and being resilient in the face of challenges. Effective communication, celebrations of milestones, and support for individual growth contribute to a partnership that not only survives but thrives. Commitment is the key that unlocks the door to a lasting, fulfilling, and ever-evolving love.

The Role of Intimacy to Satisfy a Woman

Intimacy plays a pivotal role in cementing the bonds of commitment within a relationship. Emotional and physical intimacy are both essential aspects of long-term partnerships. Emotional intimacy involves a deep connection, shared vulnerabilities, and open communication, while physical intimacy encompasses the expression of love and desire.

In a committed relationship, emotional intimacy is nurtured through shared experiences, conversations, and the willingness to be vulnerable. This emotional closeness deepens the commitment as both partners feel truly understood and cherished. It's the ability to hold each other's secrets, fears, and desires without judgment, creating a strong emotional bond.

Physical intimacy is equally important. It goes beyond the physical act of love to encompass the expression of desire, affection, and comfort through touch, hugs, and kisses. In a long-term commitment, physical intimacy reassures both partners of their attraction and emotional connection. It's a means of expressing love and desire, reinforcing their commitment to each other.

Partners who commit to each other also commit to supporting each other's passions and interests. It's about understanding that both individuals have unique aspirations and dreams outside the relationship.

For example, consider the story of Natalie and Ethan. Natalie is passionate about art, while Ethan is an avid hiker. They committed to supporting each other's interests by occasionally attending art exhibitions together and taking hiking trips. This not only allowed them to share in each other's passions but also demonstrated their commitment to each other's individual growth.

Commitment doesn't mean stagnation; it's a dynamic journey of growth together. Couples who stay committed are willing to evolve as individuals while ensuring their relationship grows alongside.

Long-term partnerships often come with their share of obstacles and conflicts. However, commitment is the driving force that compels couples to overcome these challenges.

Adaptability is Equally Important!

Adaptability is an integral part of commitment. As life changes, couples must be willing to adapt and find new ways to nurture their love.

Think of Daniel and Maria, who welcomed a child into their lives. This new responsibility required them to adapt their routines and find creative ways to keep their emotional and physical intimacy alive. Their commitment to each other and their growing family was evident in their ability to adapt, ensuring their relationship remained strong and their love deepened.

No two committed relationships are the same. Each has its unique qualities, shared jokes, and secret languages that only the couple understands. Part of the beauty of commitment is in celebrating the unique bond that you share.

Commitment doesn't always follow traditional norms or timelines. What's most important is the couple's shared understanding of their commitment to each other.

Commitment is not a one-time event but an ongoing process. Partners can renew their commitment in various ways, be it through a reaffirmation of vows, revisiting their shared vision, or making a promise to grow together.

"James and Lily, a couple married for 25 years, decided to renew their commitment by reaffirming their wedding vows in a touching ceremony. This renewal was a celebration of their journey together and a recommitment to each other for the years to come."

While commitment to each other is vital, self-commitment is equally important. In a lasting partnership, it's essential for each partner to commit to self-care.

A prime example is Chris and Sarah. They recognized that their commitment to each other was closely linked to their well-being. By committing to self-care routines, such as exercise, meditation, and maintaining personal hobbies, they not only ensured their individual happiness but also contributed to the strength of their relationship.

From Commitment to Everlasting Love

Commitment and long-term partnerships are a testament to the enduring love that couples seek. It's a journey filled with shared experiences, trials, and growth, all reinforcing the commitment between two individuals. Over time, this commitment deepens and transforms into an everlasting love that provides emotional fulfillment and unwavering support.

Commitment is the thread that weaves the fabric of lasting love. It involves a shared vision, emotional and physical intimacy, support for each other's passions, resilience in the face of obstacles, adaptability to life's changes, and a never-ending, unwritten contract of love. It's the unique bond, the celebration of the non-traditional, the renewal of vows, and a commitment to self-care that contributes to the strength of the relationship. Commitment doesn't just mark the beginning of a partnership; it's the key to everlasting love, ever-deepening and ever-thriving.

IV - All About Insecurities of Women (CFH)

Women are known for being insecure. We have a list of all the insecurities that women go through, and it's quite extensive. Let's talk about some of the common insecurities of women.Insecurities are deeply rooted in our minds. They are a part of our personality and cannot be easily erased. Insecurities, however, can be managed if one is able to accept them as a part of life.

Women tend to be more insecure than men because they want to achieve perfection in everything that they do. This trait makes them susceptible to getting hurt by the words of others or by their own actions. When women feel that they have failed at something or that they have done something wrong, they become very insecure about their actions. Women get insecure from people and situations. They're afraid that if they say no, someone will think less of them. They're afraid that if they ask for what they want, someone will reject them. They're afraid that if they fail at something, everyone will laugh at them. So instead of taking risks and being vulnerable, they play it safe, hide their true selves and hold back from being themselves.

This is the reason why women get insecure in the first place; because they're afraid of rejection and judgement from other people. So if you really want to help your girlfriend become more secure, then teach her how to handle all these situations without getting upset or nervous about them!

Women tend to get insecure about their relationships, their bodies and their lives. This is a very common human trait, but women have it in spades. Why?

The answer is that women are more relational than men. They are more connected to others in general and they feel emotions more deeply. Women also tend to be better at expressing themselves verbally, but less adept at communicating nonverbally (i.e., with their body language). This means that when women experience an emotion, they are more likely to express it verbally instead of physically or nonverbally like men do.

Women need reassurance from the people around them because they are so dependent on others for love and acceptance. This is why relationships with other people can be so important for your happiness as a woman. Your boyfriend or husband might be the most important person in your life, but if he leaves you then he takes away your happiness along with him and leaves you feeling broken inside. Your family may not mean as much to you as your boyfriend does, but if they reject you then again you feel broken inside because you no longer feel loved and accepted by those who should love and accept you unconditionally (because they're family).

Why are Women Insecure in Life?

Insecurity is a complex emotion that can affect anyone, regardless of gender. Women, however, often face unique societal pressures and expectations that can contribute to feelings of insecurity. It's important to recognize that these experiences are not universal, and many women lead confident and secure lives. Nonetheless, understanding the factors that can contribute to insecurity in some women is essential in order to address and combat this issue.

Let's explore some of the reasons why women may experience insecurity in various aspects of their lives:

- **Societal Beauty Standards:** In many societies, women are bombarded with images and messages that perpetuate narrow definitions of beauty. Media, advertising, and popular culture often promote unrealistic body ideals, leading some women to feel inadequate or insecure about their appearance. For example, the prevalence of photo-editing tools and filtered images on social media can create an unattainable standard of beauty.
- **Gender Stereotypes:** Traditional gender roles and stereotypes can also contribute to insecurity. Women have historically been assigned roles as caregivers, leading to expectations around nurturing, homemaking, and self-sacrifice. Deviating from these norms can result in criticism or judgment, which can foster insecurity in women.
- **Workplace Inequities:** In many parts of the world, women continue to face workplace inequities, including gender wage gaps, limited opportunities for advancement, and biases. These disparities can lead to professional insecurities, as women may question their worth, competence, or ability

to succeed in male-dominated fields.

- **Relationship Dynamics:** Insecurity can surface in romantic relationships. In cases of emotional or physical abuse, women may experience insecurity as a result of being controlled, manipulated, or demeaned by their partners. In healthy relationships, communication and trust are key factors in alleviating insecurities.
- **Social Expectations:** Women often juggle multiple roles and responsibilities, from career and family to social commitments. Balancing these expectations can be overwhelming, leading to feelings of inadequacy or insecurity if they perceive themselves as falling short in any area.
- **Personal Past Experiences:** Traumatic experiences such as childhood trauma, abusive relationships, or past failures can leave emotional scars that contribute to feelings of insecurity. These experiences can shape a woman's self-perception and behavior.

Some Examples for You to Understand

1. **Body Image Insecurities:** An example of the impact of beauty standards is how body image insecurities may lead to unhealthy dieting, disordered eating, or even plastic surgery in

some women, driven by a desire to conform to societal ideals.

2. **Professional Doubts:** A woman working in a male-dominated field might experience professional insecurity, doubting her capabilities due to a lack of female role models or gender bias in her workplace.
3. **Social Media Validation:** Social media can be a source of insecurity. Women might feel pressure to constantly present an idealized version of their lives, and the pursuit of likes, followers, or online validation can lead to feelings of inadequacy when these goals aren't met.

It's important to remember that insecurity is not a fixed state; it can change over time and with the right support and resourccs. Recognizing and addressing the underlying causes of insecurity is a crucial step in helping women lead more confident, secure lives. Empowerment, self-acceptance, and support systems play essential roles in alleviating these feelings of insecurity.

In these shared moments, I've realized that insecurities can stem from various sources, including family expectations, societal pressures, and the influence of friends. It's a reminder that the insecurities women face are often interconnected with a web of external factors. Recognizing these complexities allows us to approach each woman's unique journey with empathy and understanding, working together to address their insecurities and empower them to live more fulfilling and confident lives. Here are some of them mentioned you can understand below

Types of Women Insecurities

- **Insecurity from family:** A lot of women come from a family where their parents expect them to be perfect or do everything perfectly. This can make them insecure because they feel like they can't live up to their parents' expectations.
- **Insecurity from husband:** Some women feel insecure because they don't feel like they're good enough for their husband or they don't feel like they deserve him.
- **Insecurity from friends:** Some women feel insecure because they think their friends don't like them as much as other friends do, so they're jealous of other people's friendships with each other.
- **Insecurity from coworkers:** Some women feel insecure when they're at work because they think other people there are better than them at their jobs or smarter than them or more experienced than them, so they get jealous

when someone else gets promoted or gets a new job title before them.

V - THINGS WOMEN WANT BUT DONT GET IN LIFE

Women want a lot of things. They want to be loved and appreciated. They want to be respected for who they are and what they do. And, yes, they also want sex — but not as much as men think.

But here's the biggest secret of all: Women don't always know what they want.

That's right, ladies and gentlemen. Women aren't always the best at expressing their feelings or articulating their needs because they're too busy figuring those things out for themselves!

In a world where men are still the main breadwinners, women often find themselves in a position of having to take care of their family. This doesn't mean they don't want to be taken care of sometimes as well.

In the intricate tapestry of life, intimate relationships play a significant role in shaping one's sense of self, happiness, and fulfillment. For women, however, there are often unmet desires within the realm of intimacy, stemming from societal expectations, communication barriers, and evolving gender dynamics. This chapter explores various aspects of intimate expectations that women may harbor but find challenging to fulfill.

The landscape of societal expectations has undergone significant transformations over the years, yet certain gender norms persist. Men, predominantly viewed as the primary breadwinners, often hold positions of financial responsibility within the family. This dynamic can inadvertently place women in a position where they must manage familial care, which includes emotional support, childcare, and household responsibilities. However, despite these roles, women harbor the desire to be cared for and supported themselves.

This nuanced dynamic often leads to unspoken expectations within intimate relationships. While women are adept at providing care, they yearn for partners who understand the importance of reciprocity. Acknowledging these unmet desires involves dismantling traditional gender roles and fostering a more egalitarian approach to responsibilities and support within relationships.

As societal norms continue to evolve, so does the landscape of intimacy within relationships. Women, empowered by the ongoing movement for gender equality, are redefining their roles and expectations within the confines of intimate connections.

Contrary to stereotypes, women do desire sexual fulfillment, but the nature and frequency of these desires may not align with traditional expectations. It's crucial to recognize that individual preferences and needs vary widely. Some women may prioritize emotional intimacy, while others may seek more adventurous and diverse experiences.

Perhaps the most significant revelation is that women, like everyone else, don't always have a clear understanding of what they want. This isn't a shortcoming but rather a testament to the intricate and evolving nature of human desires and emotions. The journey of self-discovery is ongoing, and individuals, irrespective of gender, are continually unraveling the layers of their own desires and needs.

Navigating the unmet desires within intimate relationships for women involves a holistic approach. It requires dismantling outdated societal expectations, fostering open communication, and recognizing the evolving landscape of gender dynamics. By acknowledging and understanding these multifaceted aspects, we pave the way for healthier, more fulfilling connections where both partners can thrive in a space of mutual understanding and support.

Let's See What Women Wants and Do not Get

- **Communication and Emotional Connection:**

Effective communication is the cornerstone of any successful intimate relationship. Many women desire a deeper emotional connection with their partners, where they can openly express their thoughts, feelings, and vulnerabilities. However, societal norms often discourage men from displaying emotional sensitivity, making it challenging for women to establish the level of emotional intimacy they crave.

In fostering healthier communication, it's essential to create a space where both partners feel comfortable expressing themselves. Encouraging emotional openness, active listening, and vulnerability can contribute to a more profound connection.

- **Mutual Respect and Consent:**

Respecting boundaries and obtaining mutual consent is a fundamental aspect of any healthy relationship. Unfortunately, some women find themselves in situations where their boundaries are ignored or disrespected. Empowering women to assert their boundaries and fostering a culture of mutual respect is crucial for creating safe and fulfilling intimate connections.

Building a foundation of respect involves open communication about individual boundaries and a commitment to honoring them. Educating both partners on the importance of consent and establishing clear communication channels can contribute to a more respectful and consensual intimate relationship.

- **Equality in Pleasure:**

A common yet unspoken desire for many women is the pursuit of equality in pleasure within intimate relationships. Societal expectations and historical norms have often prioritized male pleasure, leaving women's desires and satisfaction overlooked. Emphasizing the importance of mutual pleasure and open communication about individual needs is essential for fostering a more balanced and fulfilling intimate experience.

Creating an environment where both partners prioritize each other's pleasure requires open dialogue and a willingness to explore and understand each other's desires. Encouraging a reciprocal approach to intimacy can lead to a more satisfying and equitable connection.

- **Freedom from Stigmas and Judgment:**

Societal stigmas surrounding women's sexuality can create a pervasive sense of shame and guilt. Women often desire the freedom to explore and express their sexuality without fear of judgment or societal backlash. Creating a more inclusive and sex-positive culture can empower women to embrace their sexuality authentically.

Challenging societal stigmas involves promoting education and awareness about diverse expressions of sexuality. Encouraging open conversations about sexual preferences and creating a judgment-free environment can help women feel more liberated in expressing their desires.

- **Body Positivity and Self-Confidence:**

Media portrayal of an unrealistic standard of beauty can impact women's self-esteem and body image. Many women desire acceptance and appreciation for their bodies as they are, without feeling the need to conform to societal beauty standards. Fostering a culture of body positivity and self-love is essential for women to feel confident and secure in intimate relationships.

Promoting body positivity involves celebrating diverse body types and challenging unrealistic beauty standards. Encouraging self-love and appreciation, both individually and within the relationship, can contribute to a more positive and fulfilling intimate experience.

- **Variety and Exploration:**

Intimacy is a dynamic and evolving aspect of a relationship, and women often desire variety and exploration in their intimate lives. This can include trying new things, introducing novelty, and maintaining a sense of spontaneity. Open communication about desires and preferences is crucial to ensure that both partners feel comfortable exploring new aspects of their intimacy.

Creating a sense of adventure in intimacy involves cultivating an environment where partners feel free to express their desires and fantasies without judgment. Establishing mutual trust and openness can lead to a more dynamic and satisfying intimate connection.

- **Empowerment in Sexual Decision-Making:**

Empowering women to take an active role in sexual decision-making is crucial for fostering a sense of agency and autonomy. Some women may feel pressured into conforming to traditional gender roles in the bedroom, and breaking away from these expectations can lead to more fulfilling and empowering intimate experiences.

Encouraging open discussions about sexual preferences, desires, and boundaries is vital for creating an environment where both partners actively participate in decision-making. Mutual empowerment in the bedroom can enhance the overall satisfaction and fulfillment of intimate relationships.

- **Understanding and Addressing Sexual Health:**

Addressing sexual health concerns is an integral part of maintaining a healthy intimate relationship. However, women may find it challenging to discuss such matters openly due to societal taboos or personal discomfort. Normalizing conversations about sexual health, providing adequate education, and ensuring access to healthcare resources contribute to a more supportive and informed intimate environment.

Promoting sexual health involves creating a safe space for open communication about sexual well-being. Encouraging regular check-ups, discussing contraceptive options, and addressing concerns collaboratively can contribute to a healthier and more informed intimate connection.

- **Support for Fertility Choices:**

Women's fertility choices, including decisions related to childbirth and family planning, are deeply personal. Unfortunately, societal expectations and judgments can influence these choices. Providing support and understanding for women's decisions regarding fertility, whether it involves having children or not, is essential for creating an environment where women feel empowered in their choices.

Supporting fertility choices requires open communication and a shared understanding of each partner's desires and expectations regarding family planning. Creating a supportive atmosphere where both partners feel heard and respected can contribute to a more harmonious intimate relationship.

Let's Understand this point with a Beautiful Example here -

The story of Priya and Raj, a married couple living in a small town in India. Priya, a successful professional, and Raj, an IT consultant, initially decided to focus on their careers and enjoy their newlywed life. As they approached their late twenties, discussions about family planning naturally arose.

Priya, passionate about her career and ambitions, expressed her desire to delay starting a family to achieve certain professional milestones. Raj, understanding the importance of Priya's career, supported her decision wholeheartedly. Their families, however, started expressing traditional expectations, emphasizing the societal norm of early parenthood.

In the face of societal pressures, Priya and Raj

held firm in their decision-making process. They engaged in open conversations about their goals, aspirations, and the timeline for family planning. Priya, appreciative of Raj's support, continued to pursue her career with zeal, and Raj continued to contribute to household responsibilities, creating an environment that allowed Priya to thrive professionally.

As the couple approached their thirties, Priya felt a shift in her perspective. She began contemplating the idea of parenthood, realizing that her professional achievements had provided her with a stable foundation. However, she was anxious about how her change in stance might be perceived by Raj, given their earlier decisions.

In a heartfelt conversation, Priya expressed her evolving desires to Raj, expecting potential resistance or disappointment. To her surprise, Raj not only understood but also shared in her excitement. He reassured her that their journey was about mutual growth and happiness, and they decided to explore family planning together.

The couple sought guidance from healthcare professionals to navigate the physical and emotional aspects of family planning. Priya's family, initially surprised by the change in plans, eventually embraced the couple's decision, realizing that happiness and fulfillment were not bound by societal timelines.

Priya and Raj's story reflects the challenges faced by many Indian couples in navigating the delicate balance between societal expectations and personal desires. By fostering open communication, mutual support, and adaptability, they were able to create a supportive atmosphere that allowed them to make fertility choices in line with their evolving aspirations. This example illustrates the resilience of a couple in the face of cultural expectations, emphasizing the importance of shared decision-making and mutual understanding in the Indian context.

- **Balancing Intimacy with Other Life Roles:**

Women often find themselves juggling multiple roles in life, including those of a partner, parent, professional, and caregiver. Balancing these roles while maintaining a fulfilling intimate relationship can be challenging. Recognizing and addressing the need for support, communication, and shared responsibilities is crucial for creating a sustainable and satisfying intimate partnership.

Balancing intimacy with other life roles involves acknowledging the challenges and responsibilities that each partner brings to the relationship. Establishing open communication about expectations, sharing responsibilities, and creating moments for connection amidst busy schedules can contribute to a more balanced and fulfilling intimate connection.

Intimate relationships are a vital component of a woman's life, and acknowledging and addressing unmet desires within this realm is essential for fostering healthier, more fulfilling connections. By dismantling societal expectations, promoting open communication, and embracing a more inclusive and supportive culture, we can contribute to a world where women's intimate expectations are recognized, respected, and met with understanding.

The exploration of women's unmet desires in intimate relationships has illuminated the importance of communication, understanding, and societal evolution. From desiring equal pleasure to seeking freedom from stigmas and judgment, women's intimate expectations reflect a yearning for genuine connection and fulfillment.

Societal expectations, communication barriers, and evolving gender dynamics contribute to the challenges women face in having their intimate desires recognized and fulfilled. The emphasis on breaking down traditional norms, fostering open dialogue, and creating a culture of mutual respect is essential in creating an environment where women's desires are acknowledged and met.

It is crucial to recognize that women, like everyone else, are continuously evolving, and their desires may not conform to rigid stereotypes. Building harmonious and fulfilling intimate relationships requires a commitment to mutual growth, open-mindedness, and an understanding of the individual complexities that shape desires.

In moving forward, society must strive to create spaces that empower women to express their intimate desires without fear of judgment or societal expectations. It involves dismantling stereotypes and fostering a culture that celebrates diversity in desires, preferences, and expressions of intimacy.

Ultimately, acknowledging and addressing the unmet desires of women in intimate relationships contributes to the larger narrative of gender equality. It calls for a collective effort to create a world where individuals can authentically express their desires, and where intimate connections are built on mutual understanding, respect, and a shared commitment to personal and relational growth. Through this lens, we pave the way for a more inclusive and fulfilling future, where women's desires are not only recognized but celebrated in the intricate dance of intimate connections.

PART 3: INTIMATE DESIRES OF A WOMAN

- "Creating a Safe and Comfortable Environment" - 5 pages
- "Sexual Health and Well-being" - 7 pages
- "Emotional Intimacy in the Bedroom " - 7 pages
- "Understanding Female Arousal and **Sexual Positions**" - 6 pages
- "Variety and Exploration in Intimate Life" - 5 pages

I - Creating a Safe and Comfortable Environment

The first step to having the best sex of your life is to create a safe and comfortable environment. You want to make sure that you're in a place where you feel secure and relaxed. That's why it's important to pick a location where you can be completely yourself and unapologetically express yourself physically, emotionally and intellectually.

The bedroom is often the go-to location for sexual activity, but it's not always the best choice. If you live with other people or share your space with children, it might not be appropriate for everyone involved. If this is the case, think about where else you could meet up, like at a hotel or another private location that's away from distractions (and judgment).

There are many ways you can create an intimate space that will help you both relax and feel comfortable. You can dim the lights, put on soft music and candles, or light some incense. If you don't have candles or incense, try lighting some scented candles instead — it will still set the mood. You should also make sure there is plenty of room for both of you; this way, no matter what position you're trying out, there won't be any awkwardness because one person is too close or too far away from each other.

Finally, make sure that there is nothing else distracting from the experience (i.e., no TV or computer). If there are kids or pets running around outside, put them out of sight so they won't interrupt your time together.

Once you have established a safe environment and have enough time, you need to get her talking about herself, her desires, and her fantasies. You can do this by asking questions like: "What do you like about sex?" "Is there anything that turns you on more than anything else?" "What makes a man attractive?" "What makes a woman attractive?" "Do you like foreplay?" "How long does the average man last during sex?" "How long does the average woman last during sex?"

After she answers these questions, ask some follow-up questions based on what she said: "That sounds interesting; why do women like it when men touch their breasts? Or why do men like it when women wear high heels? Or why do men prefer blowjobs over handjobs?

What is a Woman's Biggest Fear?

One of the biggest fears women have about meeting men for sex is that they will be judged. Letting your partner know that you are interested in them takes away some of that fear. Keep the conversation light, fun and flirty. If you make her laugh, she's going to feel more comfortable with you. If you can make her smile, she'll be thinking about you later when she goes to bed at night.

If she asks about your job or where you live or where you went to school, this is an opportunity for you to ask about hers as well. Ask questions about things like hobbies, family or travel experiences so that both of you can find common ground and get to know each other better.

It is important to make sure your date feels safe in every way possible: physically safe and emotionally safe. Be sure to keep your hands above the table while eating so as not to make anyone feel uncomfortable; don't bring up controversial topics such as politics or religion; avoid jokes that could come across as offensive; treat everyone with respect regardless of gender identity or sexual orientation; respect boundaries.

A woman needs to feel safe and comfortable in order to enjoy intimacy with her partner. It is important that you create an environment that is free from stress and noise. If you want to make love with your partner, then you should work on making sure that there is no one else around, so that she can relax completely and be herself.

Chances are that if she feels comfortable with you, then she will also feel comfortable with the act of making love. If you want to make love with your partner, then it is important that you keep in mind these things:

Initiate the conversation about sex – women are often not very vocal about their sexual desires or fantasies. You need to initiate a conversation with them so they can tell you what they want or like most.

Create a safe environment – if there are any distractions around, then it might not be easy for her to relax completely and enjoy the experience of being intimate with you. This could mean that she might not be able to enjoy sex as much as possible.

Women need to feel safe and comfortable before they can open up and share what is going on in their lives. If you want your relationship to be intimate, then you need to create an atmosphere where she feels safe enough to open up about her fears and concerns.

The best way to do this is by creating a safe space for her. For example:

- Listen when she speaks
- Don't interrupt or criticize
- Show interest in what she has to say
- Don't judge her feelings or experiences

Here are some tips for creating this safe environment:

Be present in the moment with her. If you aren't fully present with your partner, then it's hard for her to open up because she knows that you aren't really paying attention to what she is saying. So make sure that when she talks, look at her face and listen attentively. If there are distractions around (e.g., television), turn them off so that you can focus on your partner.

Don't interrupt or criticize what she says or

how she feels about it; just let her finish speaking before responding in any way. Don't try to solve her problems right away either

My Experience to Understand Intimate Desires

I've always loved my job as a sex therapist. I'm very open-minded, and I enjoy helping people explore their sexuality. My patients are all of different ages and backgrounds, but they have one thing in common: they're each dealing with issues of intimacy, intimacy that they often feel they can't share with anyone else.

Each week, I have an opportunity to listen to these people's stories and help them live their best lives. But it wasn't always this way. When I first started working in the field of sex therapy, I jumped at the chance to learn more about how to help others with their intimate issues.

I'd always been interested in helping others improve their lives, so being a sex therapist seemed like the perfect fit for me. It was something that would allow me to work with people on an intimate level while also teaching them things they might not have known before.

Many women suffer from intimacy issues because of shame or embarrassment around sex itself - whatever their problem may be they're afraid that if they talk about.

After all such experiences I decided it was time for a change. It wasn't that I didn't like helping women; quite the opposite — I loved being able to empower them and teach them how to stand up for themselves when faced with challenging situations. But it wasn't enough for me anymore; there was something missing from my life, something that went beyond helping other people find happiness and fulfillment through counseling sessions every week or so!

Intimacy is a complicated thing. We all have our own ideas about what it means to be intimate with someone, and we each have our own unique needs when it comes to emotional and physical connection. It can be difficult to find the right person who understands these needs and wants to meet them.

We all want different things from our relationships, but there are some common threads that run through most people's desires. Here are some of the most common intimate desires that I've seen in my patients over the years:

1. **A desire for companionship**
2. **A desire for emotional intimacy**
3. **A desire for sex**

Once you've established trust with your partner, it's time to talk about what you want from each other. This can be difficult for some people because they are afraid of rejection or embarrassment, but if you have already created a safe space then there is no need to worry about either one happening! Be open and honest with each other about what makes you tick. If there are certain things that turn you on that might seem strange or weird then just say so! Remember that this is all about having fun with each other so don't take anything too seriously!

In order to experience true intimacy, it is important that both parties feel safe and comfortable with one another. If you are unsure about how to create this environment. When you love someone, it is easy to take them for granted. However, when it comes to intimacy, there are things that need to be said out loud so that both partners are on the same page. Take time out of each day to tell your partner how much he means to you and how much you appreciate his efforts at home and in life in general (if he needs some work). It's important that you communicate all of this verbally. When you show love through actions rather than words, it is sometimes hard for your partner to understand what is going on inside of you or if there is anything wrong at all because they cannot hear or understand what's being said with words alone.

A woman may be worried about whether or not she will be hurt during sex or if her partner will try to force her into something that she does not want to do. Similarly, a man may be concerned about his own physical well-being and whether or not he can trust the woman he is with. A good way to build trust between two people is by creating an environment that feels safe for both partners. This can include everything from making sure there are no distractions around (e.g., your phone ringing) to having the lights turned down low so that you won't feel exposed by bright lights.

Always remember, a woman needs to feel safe in order to explore her intimate desires. If she's not comfortable in the environment you're providing, she's not going to be able to relax and get into the mood.

II - Understanding Sexual Health and Well-Being of a Woman (CFH)

In this part of the book, you will learn about the importance of sex. You will also learn how to create a healthy sexual relationship with your partner.

The topic of sexual health is extremely important, as it is a vital part of our lives. In this section, you will learn about the different aspects of sexuality and how they can impact our lives.

Sexual health is important because it affects our overall well-being in many different ways. For example, if someone has sexual dysfunction or a disability, they may not be able to engage in sexual activity at all or they may experience pain during intercourse. This can lead to depression or other mental health issues if left untreated.

In addition to this, there are many other factors that affect our overall well-being when it comes to sex and intimacy with another person.

For example: age, gender identity, race/ ethnicity and socioeconomic status can all impact how we perceive ourselves sexually and how we interact with others intimately as well..

Sexual health and well-being of a woman is vital to her overall health and quality of life. Sexuality is not just about sex, but it's also about love, intimacy, closeness and vulnerability. Female sexuality is complex and multi-dimensional. It involves physical, emotional, psychological and social aspects.

A woman's sexual health and well-being are affected by many factors. The following are some of them that I have seen in people over the years.

The Sexual Health and Well-being of a woman is an ever evolving process. A woman's sexuality is affected by her present situation, her past experiences, her culture and the society in which she lives. A woman's body changes with age and hormonal fluctuations also affect sexual response.

- **Mental Health:** A woman's mental health affects her sexual health because it can affect her mood, which could make it difficult for her to relax enough for sex. If she is depressed or anxious about something else, this can also affect how much pleasure she gets from sex or how often she wants to have sex with her partner(s).
- **Intimate relationships:** A woman's intimate relationships affect her sexual health because they play an important role in how comfortable and relaxed she feels around people who are close to her. This includes romantic partners, family members, friends and other people in a woman's life who care about her well-being (such as doctors and therapists).
- **Physical Factors:**
    - ❖ Health Conditions: Certain medical conditions, such as diabetes, multiple sclerosis, or chronic pain, can impact a woman's sexual well-being. These conditions can lead to physical discomfort, pain during intercourse, or fatigue.

- ❖ Medications: Some medications, including antidepressants, antihypertensives, or birth control pills, can have side effects that affect sexual desire or function. Discussing potential side effects with a healthcare provider is important.

- ❖ Pregnancy and Postpartum Changes: The physical and hormonal changes that occur during pregnancy and after childbirth can impact a woman's sexual well-being. These changes may include body image concerns, hormonal fluctuations, or physical discomfort

- **Age Factors:** The sexual health of a woman is affected by age as well as hormones. Changes in hormone levels cause vaginal lubrication, arousal and orgasm to decrease over time as she ages due to decreased blood flow to these areas of her body resulting from decreased estrogen levels after menopause.

- **Relationship status:** The relationship status of a woman, whether she is single or married, can have a profound influence on her intimate life and how willing she is to explore her desires and communicate her needs. Single women may face uncertainties in the dating world. Trust, open communication, and physical comfort can be challenging to establish, especially in the early stages of dating. Despite independence, single women may desire a deep emotional and physical connection. Finding a partner who can provide both can be a challenge.

- **Hormonal Factors**
  - Menstrual Cycle: Hormonal fluctuations throughout the menstrual cycle can affect a woman's sexual desire and responsiveness. Some women may experience heightened desire during certain phases, while others may experience changes in libido.
  - Menopause: The hormonal changes that accompany menopause, such as a decline in estrogen levels, can lead to physical changes that affect sexual comfort and function. These changes may include vaginal dryness and decreased libido.

A Path to Understand Female Body and Desires

There are many reasons a woman may not have an orgasm, but the most common one is that a man's technique needs to be improved.

A woman's sexual response is complicated and unique to her own body. It's important for husbands to understand this process and how they can help their wives experience pleasure and intimacy.

The female orgasm is often misunderstood as a series of steps or stages that lead up to the big "O." But there really isn't a formulaic path that all women follow when they climax. Some women find their first orgasm during masturbation; others don't experience one until they're in their 30s or 40s — or never at all.

The key to having better sex is understanding how your wife's body works and what she likes in bed, which can require an open mind and some trial and error on both sides.

To understand her sexual health better, here are some facts:

- Sexual health is not just about performing well in bed. It is more than that. It is about feeling comfortable with one's body and sexuality.
- Sexual health encompasses many aspects like emotional, physical and mental aspects of a woman and her partner's life together.
- The intimate desires of a woman are unique to her and only she knows what really excites her!
- The first step to understanding your wife's needs sexually is to ask how she feels about herself as a woman. You should ask her how she feels about her body as well as how much

she enjoys sex with you.

- A lot of men think that if they talk about sex too much then it will make their wives uncomfortable or even lose interest in sex altogether – but nothing could be further from the truth! In fact, it will only make things better between you two!

Understanding Common Sexual Health Concerns of Women

Women are often hesitant to talk about sexual concerns with their healthcare provider. A recent survey found that only 25 percent of women discussed sexual problems with their doctor or other healthcare provider in the past year. The most common reason for not discussing this topic is embarrassment or fear of being judged. While there is no shame in asking for help, it's important to understand the common sexual health concerns of women and what you can do about them.The following are some of the most common sexual health concerns of women. It's important to note that while these issues can be a source of distress, they don't necessarily mean there is something wrong with you.

- **Many Women have Lack of desire:** This may be due to stress, fatigue, or other factors. If it's been going on for a long time, you should see your doctor for an evaluation.

- **Women Face Pain during intercourse:** Painful intercourse can be caused by vaginal dryness or irritation from spermicides, latex condoms or diaphragms. It can also be a sign of infection or another medical problem. If you're having pain during sex, talk to your doctor.
- **Alot of Women have Low libido:** Sometimes low libido is related to life stressors like depression or anxiety, but it can also be caused by hormonal changes related to menopause or birth control pills. Talk to your doctor if you're having trouble arousing yourself sexually and want advice about treatment options such as hormone therapy
- **Vaginal infections:** These include bacterial vaginosis, trichomoniasis (Trich) and candidiasis (yeast). These infections can cause itching, burning and discharge from the vagina. It's also possible for women to have more than one infection at one time.
- **Pain During Intercourse:** Pain during intercourse or other sexual activities, including painful sex, can be a challenging issue that many individuals, both women and men, may encounter in their intimate relationships. One significant but often misunderstood cause of painful sex is vaginismus, a condition that

can affect women. However, it's important to highlight that many male partners may not be aware of or fully understand this problem, which can lead to misconceptions and emotional challenges within a relationship.

Women enjoy being touched in different places on their bodies. So, before going for a sexual encounter with your lady love, it is important that you learn about her body first. If she loves being touched on her back or neck then do not hesitate in doing so while having sex with her! Also, make sure that you do not rush into anything as it would ruin the mood completely!

III - Emotional Intimacy in the Bedroom

"Emotional Intimacy in the Bedroom" refers to the deep emotional connection and closeness between partners during sexual encounters and activities. It's about more than just physical pleasure; it involves a profound emotional bond that enhances the overall quality of the intimate experience. Here's an explanation of the key elements within this concept:

1. Trust and Vulnerability:

Emotional intimacy hinges on trust and the ability to be vulnerable with your partner. In the context of the bedroom, trust means feeling safe enough to open up about your desires, fears, and insecurities.

It's the assurance that your partner will respect your vulnerability and won't exploit it. This trust allows for the freedom to explore your emotional and sexual needs without apprehension.

2. Safe and Comfortable Environment:

Creating a safe space in the bedroom is paramount for emotional intimacy. This involves ensuring that the physical environment is comfortable and free from distractions. But more importantly, it's about the psychological environment where partners feel emotionally safe. This emotional sanctuary is devoid of judgment or criticism, where both partners can express themselves honestly.

3. Emotional Needs and Fulfillment:

Emotional intimacy is about recognizing and responding to each other's emotional needs. It's not just about physical pleasure but ensuring that both partners feel emotionally fulfilled during intimate encounters. This requires active communication and attentiveness to each other's desires and boundaries.

4. Deeper Emotional Connection:

During emotionally intimate moments, partners are not solely focused on the physical act but also on the emotional connection they share. They are attuned to each other's feelings and respond to each other's emotional cues. This deep emotional connection heightens the overall quality of the intimate experience, making it more meaningful and fulfilling.

5. Affection and Romance:

Affection and romance play a significant role in emotional intimacy. These aspects extend beyond the bedroom and include gestures of love and affection in daily life. Engaging in activities that foster emotional closeness, such as cuddling, hugging, or sharing heartfelt conversations, enhances the emotional bond between partners. This emotional connection naturally carries over into intimate moments, making them more profound.

6. Overcoming Challenges:

Challenges may arise that can hinder emotional intimacy in the bedroom. These might include personal insecurities, external stressors, or unresolved relationship issues. Overcoming these challenges involves working together as a team. Partners need to actively address and resolve any emotional or relational obstacles that may impede their connection.

7. Meaningful and Satisfying Encounters:

Emotional intimacy is the secret ingredient that can

transform physical encounters into meaningful and deeply satisfying experiences. It's about feeling connected on a profound level, emotionally and physically. When emotional intimacy is present, the physical aspect of intimacy is more fulfilling and enjoyable.

In essence, emotional intimacy in the bedroom is about merging the physical and emotional aspects of intimacy to create an all-encompassing, deeply connected experience. It's not just about sex but about feeling emotionally close, secure, and understood by your partner during these moments. Cultivating emotional intimacy can lead to more meaningful and satisfying intimate encounters, strengthening the bond between partners.

IV - Understanding Female Arousal and Sexual Positions

Sex is a beautiful thing, but it's not always easy to get the most out of it.

Many men aren't sure what women really want in bed. And while they may think they know, they're often wrong!

As a woman who has been in a relationship for over 10 years now, I can tell you that there are some things every man needs to know about satisfying your lady. If you want her to crave sex with you and want more of it, then these tips will help you take your relationship to the next level.

A woman's arousal cycle begins in her brain. She may not be aware of it, but her mind plays a big role in what makes her sexually excited.

Arousal starts with a thought or fantasy. **For example,** she might have the desire to have sex with someone or something. This desire eventually moves through her body and causes certain physical changes. Her heart rate increases and blood flows to her genitals, which become swollen and sensitive to touch.

If she feels safe and comfortable, then she may allow herself to feel pleasure from the physical stimulation of sexual contact. If she doesn't feel safe or comfortable, then she might not allow herself to experience an orgasm (or any type of sexual pleasure).

Arousal is a process that can happen very quickly or very slowly over time depending on each woman's unique needs and desires at any given moment in time.

So what are the secret desires of a woman?

We've all heard about the man's "pleasure points", but what about the woman's? A woman might not need to be touched in certain places to get aroused, but she does have her own special hot spots that will make her feel good.

One of the secret desires of a woman is for her partner to know exactly how to pleasure her. The more he knows about how she likes to be touched and stimulated, the better. He should also be willing to learn from her or from other sources (like books or videos) so he can give her exactly what she wants.

Asking questions is always a good way to start learning about this topic. Don't be afraid to ask your partner what she likes most; don't assume that she'll automatically know what you like best either! It's important that both partners are satisfied during intimate moments together if they want their relationship to last long term. Female arousal is a complex process that varies from woman to woman.

“There are several factors that can affect a woman’s desire for sex, including”

- ❖ Her level of desire for you. If she’s crazy about you, she’ll be much more likely to get aroused by seeing you undressed or touching her body.
- ❖ Her general feelings about sex. Some women get turned on by sexual fantasies or porn while others are more interested in the emotional aspects of intimacy. Her physical condition at the time. If she’s

tired or stressed out, she may not be capable of getting aroused enough to enjoy sex fully.

- Her mental state at the time. If she's distracted by something else going on in her life (like an argument with her boss), it will be harder to get in the mood for lovemaking than if she were focused solely on you and what you were doing together.
- When she is stressed or anxious, it can be hard to relax enough to enjoy sex. This is especially true if you're worried about things like money or work. The more you worry, the less likely it is that you will want to have sex.

V - Variety and Exploration in Intimate Life of a Woman

The intimate life of a woman is a multifaceted and ever-evolving aspect of her identity. It goes beyond the physical aspects of intimacy, encompassing emotional connections, effective communication, and personal growth. Embracing variety and exploration in a woman's intimate life is pivotal to breaking free from societal constraints and rigid expectations. By challenging traditional norms, women can embark on a journey of self-discovery and empowerment that allows them to explore new avenues of pleasure, communication, and connection.

"A Multidimensional Approach to Intimacy"

Intimacy is not a one-dimensional concept; it's a multifaceted jewel with many facets. Women experience intimacy on physical, emotional, and psychological levels. Variety and exploration allow women to traverse these intricate paths, unlocking the doors to profound connections and experiences.

Physical intimacy is the aspect most commonly associated with the word "intimate." It involves touch, closeness, and shared moments of vulnerability. But there's more to it than meets the eye. In the context of variety and exploration, physical intimacy can encompass not only traditional forms of physical connection but also more unconventional or creative expressions of desire and affection.

Emotional intimacy, on the other hand, delves into the depths of one's feelings and connections. It's the ability to be open, vulnerable, and empathetic with a partner. By exploring different emotional dimensions, women can create a more profound emotional connection, fostering trust and understanding.

Psychological intimacy involves the exploration of one's fantasies, desires, and psychological needs. This aspect is often overlooked but can significantly impact a woman's intimate life. Variety and exploration in the psychological realm allow women to understand themselves better, embrace their unique desires, and communicate them to their partners.

"Mindful Communication: The Key to Connection"

Effective communication lies at the heart of any successful intimate relationship. When it comes to variety and exploration, mindful communication takes center stage. This involves a comprehensive approach to expressing needs, desires, and boundaries to enhance understanding and connection.

Explicit conversations about desires, boundaries, and fantasies are a fundamental part of mindful communication. By openly discussing these topics, women can create a safe space where their partners understand their preferences and boundaries. It also encourages their partners to share their own desires and boundaries, promoting a sense of reciprocity and mutual respect.

Non-verbal communication is equally essential. Actions often speak louder than words, and non-verbal cues can profoundly impact an intimate connection. Simple gestures like tender touch, lingering eye contact, or a warm smile can convey love, passion, and understanding. By embracing non-verbal communication, women can deepen their emotional connection with their partners.

"Sexual Empowerment: Reclaiming Control"

Variety and exploration in intimate life empower women to regain control over their sexuality. In many societies, the narrative surrounding female sexuality has been limited and often dictated by external influences. However, by exploring their desires and boundaries, women can take back ownership of their pleasure and satisfaction.

Self-discovery is a vital component of sexual empowerment. Understanding one's body, desires, and what brings pleasure is a journey of self-empowerment. It allows women to communicate their needs more effectively to their partners and advocate for their own satisfaction.

Exploring new experiences is another aspect of sexual empowerment. Whether it's trying different sexual positions, experimenting with new activities, or introducing novelty into the relationship, women can take charge of their intimate experiences and explore the full spectrum of pleasure.

"Couple Exploration: Deepening Emotional Bonds"

Variety and exploration are not solo endeavors. They also involve partners embarking on a journey of discovery together. In the context of a relationship, embracing variety and exploration can lead to heightened emotional intimacy and fulfillment.

Couples who explore new dimensions of intimacy together often experience a more profound emotional connection. Sharing new experiences, desires, and fantasies strengthens their bond. It fosters trust, promotes mutual understanding, and enhances their emotional connection.

Creating a safe space for open communication within a relationship is crucial. Partners should feel comfortable sharing their desires and boundaries. By doing so, they can create a non-judgmental environment that supports variety and exploration.

"Personal Growth: The Journey of Self-Discovery"

Variety and exploration in intimate life contribute significantly to personal growth. It allows women to explore new dimensions of themselves and their desires. This knowledge enables them to evolve continuously, both as individuals and as partners.

Self-discovery is an ongoing process that promotes personal growth. It involves understanding one's evolving desires, boundaries, and preferences. It's about recognizing how one changes over time and being open to exploring new facets of one's identity.

Personal growth also encompasses a woman's evolving role within a relationship. As a partner, she learns how to communicate more effectively, advocate for her desires, and create a fulfilling intimate life. These skills contribute to her personal growth and enable her to enrich her partnership.

Embracing variety and exploration in a woman's intimate life is not about breaking free from tradition for the sake of novelty. It's about self-discovery, empowerment, and the profound connections that come from understanding one's own desires and boundaries.

Variety and exploration lead to more profound connections on physical, emotional, and psychological levels. They encourage mindful communication that enhances understanding and connection with a partner. They empower women to reclaim control over their own satisfaction, and they deepen emotional bonds within a relationship.

Personal growth is the natural outcome of this journey, allowing women to continuously evolve and enrich their intimate lives. It's a celebration of individuality and partnership.

PART 4: EMPOWERING WOMEN'S DESIRES

I - Breaking Stereotypes and Overcoming Stigmas: Empowering Women's Desires

Stereotypes and stigmas surrounding women's sexual desires have persisted for generations, imposing a range of restrictions and judgments. Empowering women to fully embrace and express their desires requires challenging these deeply ingrained notions. In this exploration, we will delve into the importance of breaking stereotypes and overcoming stigmas as crucial steps in the journey toward empowering women's desires.

The Landscape of Stereotypes

Stereotypes have a profound influence on our perception of what women should desire, especially in the context of intimate relationships. Society often adheres to traditional gender roles that dictate expectations, and these expectations can vary across different cultures and generations. Such stereotypes can lead to a narrow view of women's desires, hindering their ability to express themselves openly.

One critical aspect of breaking stereotypes is understanding that there is no universal or one-size-fits-all definition of what women should desire. Just as with men, women's desires are incredibly diverse, and they vary significantly from one individual to another. The spectrum of desires encompasses emotional connection, physical intimacy, various forms of arousal, and a multitude of preferences in sexual activity. Empowering women means acknowledging and embracing this diversity.

Breaking Stereotypes and Overcoming Stigmas - Embracing Intimate Desires

Sexuality has been stigmatized throughout history, and women's desires have not been exempt from these societal judgments. Stigmas surrounding women's sexual desires can lead to feelings of shame, guilt, and repression. Overcoming these stigmas is a critical step in the journey to empower women to fully express their desires.

In a world where societal norms and stereotypes have often imposed restrictions and judgment upon women's sexual desires, it's essential to challenge these preconceived notions and create a space for women to explore and express their desires freely. Breaking stereotypes and overcoming stigmas isn't just a social endeavor; it's deeply intimate and personal.

The Weight of Sexual Stigma in Women

Sexual stigma carries a heavy weight. It lurks in the shadows, whispering tales of what is "appropriate" or "acceptable." These whispers can be particularly insidious for women, influencing not just how they express their desires but even how they perceive them. Breaking free from this burden is a journey that women must embark on to embrace the full spectrum of their desires.

For many, sexual stigma is a nagging voice that whispers in the back of their minds, casting doubts on their desires and preferences. It can manifest as shame, insecurity, or fear of judgment. But as women begin to confront and challenge these stigmas, they open the door to a world of self-acceptance, empowerment, and intimate fulfillment.

Diverse Desires, Individual Paths

Breaking stereotypes involves recognizing that there's no one-size-fits-all definition of what women should desire. Women, like men, have diverse desires, and these can vary widely from person to person. Embracing this diversity means acknowledging that there's no "normal" when it comes to intimate desires. Every woman's journey is unique, and her desires are a reflection of her individuality.

The intimate touch in breaking stereotypes and overcoming stigmas lies in understanding that every woman's intimate desires are valid and should be celebrated. By acknowledging and respecting this diversity, we create an environment where women can express their desires without fear of judgment or ridicule. It's about validating the intimate path each woman chooses to walk.

Overcoming stigmas means acknowledging that there's no shame in wanting and enjoying a fulfilling intimate life. Women should never feel guilty for pursuing their desires and seeking pleasure. Yet, societal norms and stereotypes have often labeled these desires as taboo, leading to a culture of judgment and shame.

Breaking free from this judgment is a deeply intimate act. It's about understanding that one's desires are a natural part of their identity. It's embracing the truth that seeking pleasure and fulfillment is a fundamental human experience. By casting aside the cloak of shame and judgment, women can step into a world where their intimate desires are embraced and celebrated.

One way to break stereotypes and overcome stigmas is through education and open dialogue. Knowledge is a powerful tool in dispelling myths and misconceptions surrounding intimate desires. By providing accurate information about sexuality and desires, we can empower women to challenge preconceived notions.

Within these intimate dialogues, the **power**

of sexual understanding plays a pivotal role. Partners who are willing to learn about each other's desires, preferences, and fantasies demonstrate not only empathy but also a deep commitment to their relationship's intimate well-being. This level of understanding encompasses a willingness to explore new experiences, experiment with desires, and genuinely invest in their partner's satisfaction.

Men can play a significant role in this process by actively seeking to understand their **partner's sexual needs**. It involves inquiring, listening, and responding with an open heart. By being attuned to their partner's desires, men can create a safe and accepting space for women to fully embrace their intimate desires. This process of understanding not only fosters trust and connection but also fuels **sexual satisfaction.**

The Power of Personal Stories of Women

Empowering women to speak up about their desires and experiences is another vital step in breaking stereotypes and overcoming stigmas. Personal stories are deeply intimate, and they hold the potential to inspire and resonate with others. By sharing their stories and experiences, women can help others realize they're not alone in their desires and that it's perfectly acceptable to seek fulfillment.

In intimate relationships, sharing personal stories can create a profound sense of connection and trust. Partners who open up about their desires and experiences demonstrate vulnerability and acceptance. They create a safe space for each other to explore and express their intimate desires freely. The power of personal stories in an intimate context is immeasurable, as it strengthens the emotional bonds between partners.

Breaking stereotypes and overcoming stigmas is an ongoing process that involves societal change, but it starts with individuals challenging these norms in their daily lives. On an intimate level, this means embracing vulnerability and freedom in expressing desires without fear.

By rejecting stereotypes, women can reclaim their intimate desires as a powerful aspect of their identity. This intimate journey involves embracing vulnerability, sharing personal stories, and engaging in open dialogue with partners. It's about challenging preconceived notions and recognizing the validity of every woman's individual desires. In doing so, women can create a deeply intimate and fulfilling relationship with their own desires and with their partners.

II - Consent and Boundaries

Consent and boundaries are fundamental to any

healthy and fulfilling intimate relationship. They serve as the pillars on which trust and respect are built. This chapter will delve into the critical aspects of consent and boundaries, emphasizing their importance and how they contribute to a woman's empowerment in her intimate life.

Consent is a voluntary, enthusiastic, and clear agreement between all involved parties to engage in a specific activity. It is an ongoing process that can be withdrawn at any point. Consent is not just a formality but an essential aspect of a healthy intimate life. It ensures that all parties feel comfortable, respected, and safe.

Respecting boundaries is equally crucial. Boundaries define personal limits and comfort zones, both physically and emotionally. It's essential to communicate openly with a partner about individual boundaries, understand and respect them, and create a safe space for both partners to express their desires.

When it comes to empowering women's desires, the concept of enthusiastic consent is vital. It means that both partners should actively and eagerly participate in intimate activities. Encouraging open communication about desires, preferences, and boundaries fosters mutual respect and understanding. The emphasis should be on the importance of ongoing communication and checking in with each other to ensure that both partners are comfortable and satisfied.

III - Self-Exploration and Self-Confidence in Women

Self-exploration and self-confidence are powerful tools for women to enhance their intimate lives. It involves getting to know one's own desires, preferences, and fantasies. By exploring personal desires, women can reclaim control over their intimate experiences and develop self-confidence in their sexual identity.

Women often face societal pressures and stigmas regarding their sexual desires and bodies. Self-exploration is a means of breaking free from these constraints. It involves understanding one's own body and what brings pleasure. This knowledge empowers women to communicate their needs and desires to their partners confidently.

Self-confidence plays a crucial role in a woman's intimate life. It is essential to feel comfortable in one's own skin and embrace one's unique desires. Building self-confidence involves recognizing that there is no one-size-fits-all approach to intimacy and that each individual's desires are valid.

IV - Encouraging Open Conversations

Open conversations are the foundation of a healthy intimate relationship. Encouraging dialogue about desires, concerns, and boundaries allows partners to connect on a deeper level and create a safe and open environment. Open conversations are an opportunity for partners to share their fantasies and desires without judgment. It is a chance to learn about each other's preferences and make adjustments to ensure a satisfying and fulfilling intimate life.

Creating a culture of open conversations in an **intimate relationship** means establishing trust, vulnerability, and a non-judgmental attitude. Encouraging partners to express their desires freely, knowing that they will be heard and respected, is key to a strong and empowering intimate life.

One way to empower women's desires is to create a culture of sexual communication. Partners should feel safe and comfortable discussing their sexual needs, preferences, and fantasies. Encouraging open conversations about sexuality allows women and their partners to explore their desires together.

Encouraging discussions about sexual desires and preferences enables women to express their needs and helps partners understand and meet those needs. Women should feel empowered to communicate what brings them pleasure and satisfaction in intimate moments. By doing so, they can guide their partners to provide the desired experiences.

For men, supporting their female partners in this journey of self-discovery and open communication is a crucial aspect of fostering an enriching **intimate life**. Being attentive and responsive to their partners' desires not only enhances the overall experience but also strengthens the emotional connection between partners. The road to open conversations about sexuality and intimacy may involve breaking down stigmas and dispelling myths that have surrounded these subjects. As women and their partners engage in open and honest dialogue, they can challenge societal norms that have imposed restrictions on their sexual desires.

Overcoming sexual stigmas allows women to embrace their sexuality without shame or guilt. It is essential for women to understand that their desires are natural and valid, and they should not feel judged or constrained in expressing them.

Partners should actively listen to what their female partners have to say. It's not just about hearing words; it's about truly understanding and empathizing with their thoughts, feelings, and desires. When a partner listens attentively, it fosters a sense of emotional closeness and reassurance for women.Encouraging women to express themselves openly and honestly requires the active support of their partners.

Creating an environment where women feel safe to express their thoughts, desires, and boundaries is a shared responsibility. This support helps women overcome any reluctance or fear they might have about discussing intimate matters.

THE CLIMAX - "EMPOWERING WOMEN TO EXPRESS THEIR SEXUAL DESIRES"

Empowering women to express their sexual desires is a transformative and intimate journey that transcends the physical realm, delving deep into the core of human connection. In a world where sexual desires are often shrouded in stigma and misconceptions, empowering women to embrace and articulate their sexual fantasies, preferences, and needs becomes an essential step toward personal liberation and relational fulfillment.

Sexual desires are intricate, multifaceted layers of yearning that evolve with time, experiences, and emotional connections. Empowering women to express their sexual desires starts with acknowledging and accepting this complexity. Partners can create an atmosphere of acceptance and understanding, where women feel safe to peel back the layers and explore the depths of their desires without fear of judgment.

Consider a scenario where Maya, a woman in a loving relationship with her partner, Alex, feels a mix of curiosity and apprehension about her sexual desires. Alex approaches this delicate conversation with patience and an open mind. He listens as Maya articulates her desires, allowing her the freedom to express even the most intricate facets of her fantasies. This act of unconditional acceptance creates a profound intimacy, fostering trust and allowing Maya to embrace her desires with confidence.

Empowering women to express their sexual desires involves fostering open and honest dialogue. Partners can initiate conversations where women feel encouraged to vocalize their needs, explore their fantasies, and discuss their boundaries openly. This open dialogue is not only a pathway to understanding desires but also a way to deepen emotional intimacy.cPartners play a pivotal role in building this foundation. When women know they are respected, cherished, and desired, they gain the confidence to voice their intimate needs openly. Partners can express their admiration for each other's bodies, creating an environment where self-assurance and **sexual confidence** can flourish.

Moreover, Empowering women to express their sexual desires often involves embracing vulnerability. Partners can encourage this vulnerability by reciprocating trust and openness. When both partners are willing to reveal their desires and vulnerabilities, it creates a reciprocal atmosphere of trust and acceptance. **Every woman's sexual desires are unique, shaped by personal experiences, fantasies, and emotional connections.** Empowering women involves celebrating this individuality. Partners can acknowledge and embrace the distinctiveness of their loved one's desires, understanding that these desires are an integral part of their identity.

The beauty of this collaborative effort lies in the symphony it creates. The desires of women harmonize with the love and understanding of their partners, weaving a tapestry of passion, trust, and unending fulfillment. It's a tale where every partner plays an integral role, where desires and dreams entwine, culminating in a crescendo of profound connection and the celebration of human love in all its forms.

It involves creating a space where women feel secure, respected, and valued. Partners who embark on this journey together strengthen their bond, deepen their emotional intimacy, and pave the way for a mutually satisfying and fulfilling intimate life. It's a celebration of love, desire, and the profound connection that makes every moment shared between partners truly extraordinary.

Empowering women to express their sexual desires is a collaborative effort. Men can be partners in this journey, contributing to the creation of a space where women are free to explore and articulate their desires. In embracing their authentic selves, women empower themselves and their partners, ultimately contributing to a world where intimate desires are celebrated and honored.

As the final words of this book caress the page, it's a reminder that the empowerment of **women's sexual desires** is not just a chapter but an ongoing story. It's a journey where every woman is the protagonist, where every partner is a co-author. Together, they script a tale of intimacy, passion, and liberation, embracing the boundless beauty of human connection.